STRIVING FOR EQUITY

STRIVING FOR EQUITY

*District Leadership for Narrowing
Opportunity and Achievement Gaps*

Robert G. Smith
S. David Brazer

Harvard Education Press
Cambridge, Massachusetts

Library of Congress Control Number 2015955542

Paperback ISBN 978-1-61250-937-2
Library Edition ISBN 978-1-61250-938-9

Published by Harvard Education Press,
an imprint of the Harvard Education Publishing Group

Harvard Education Press
8 Story Street
Cambridge, MA 02138

Cover Design: Habib J. Dean

The typefaces used in this book are Adobe Garamond Pro and Futura

We dedicate this volume to the thirteen superintendents for whom our admiration and appreciation increased as we worked on this project. Brazer also dedicates this book to Larry Cuban—friend, mentor, exemplary superintendent; and Smith dedicates it to his wife, Sandra, who has provided support for over fifty years, and to his daughters, Heather and Pamela.

Contents

Introduction

"The education system in the United States is broken." When that phrase is entered into a Google search, it yields nearly forty-five million results. Websites on the first two pages alone embrace arguments on all sides of the statement. It's true—large numbers of students are denied access to meaningful education. Yet we believe that this declaration is a gross generalization, drawn from specific cases of egregious failures in school districts and schools. The main problem with the "system is broken" argument is that it creates a sense that all public schools are hopelessly flawed—that they merely warehouse students and provide paychecks for teachers and administrators who go through the motions with minimal effort each school day. Those who claim our schools are broken call for the nation to clear away traditional K–12 schools and rebuild the system from the ground up.

In particular, critics point to achievement gaps based on race or ethnicity, income, dominant language, and disabilities. Eliminating them has been a major national educational priority for over a decade, enshrined in No Child Left Behind (NCLB) and in subsequent initiatives such as Race to the Top. Despite this national legislative and executive priority and the testing regimens, sanctions, and incentives directed at the problem of achievement gaps, national progress overall has been at best halting, with the degree of gap closing slight and distributed unevenly across individual schools and school districts.[1]

In most of the 13,500 school districts and more than 132,000 schools in the United States, the system is *not* broken.[2] While there is much that is indefensible in public education, there are education leaders who are striving and succeeding in their efforts to improve educational equity in

1

the face of enormous challenges. In this book, we present one group of thirteen superintendents who have cut across the grain of disappointing results to make progress in closing opportunity and achievement gaps under the institutionalized constraints of traditional public school systems. Our mission is to tease out what can be learned from the practice and experiences of district superintendents who have devoted their careers to closing those gaps.

WHO WE ARE

Both of us were school practitioners before we became university professors. Smith spent forty-four years working in three school districts (Frederick County, Maryland; Spring Independent School District, Houston, Texas; and Arlington Public Schools, Arlington, Virginia). He taught high school social studies, led an adult and a junior high school, served in a variety of central office roles in Frederick, ranging from adult education to director of curriculum and staff development, worked for sixteen years as the assistant superintendent of curriculum and instructional services in the Spring Independent School District, and retired from preK–12 education after twelve years as the superintendent of the Arlington Public Schools. He joined Brazer on the faculty of the Education Leadership Program at George Mason University in Fairfax, Virginia, in the 2009–2010 school year. He was one of the fourteen original members of the governing board of the Minority Student Achievement Network (MSAN) and with five colleagues authored the book *Gaining on the Gap: Changing Hearts, Minds and Practice*, a reflection on the Arlington Public School's experiences with narrowing achievement gaps.[3]

Brazer spent fifteen years as a middle and high school teacher and administrator, serving the last six years of his K–12 career as principal of Los Altos High School in Los Altos, California. He joined the faculty of George Mason University in 1999. In June 2013, Brazer accepted a position as an associate professor and faculty director of Leadership Degree Programs at Stanford University.

OUR STUDY OF SCHOOL DISTRICT SUPERINTENDENTS

Shrinking the achievement gaps between minority and majority populations in school districts is critical to achieving equitable outcomes in education. A great deal has been published about the nature, depth, and duration of achievement gaps, but superintendents' efforts and perspectives have been little explored.[4] It is with this in mind that we designed the study on which this book is based. Our intent was to learn more about apparently successful school districts and their leaders who seemed to buck the disappointing national trend of slow or no progress when it came to closing gaps. We wanted to learn what made them different, and we believed that the best way to learn how they approached the issue of closing gaps would be to talk to them directly and use their words as the basis for our analysis.

The study was planned during the 2009–2010 school year. It centered largely on interviews of thirteen school district superintendents, all of whom were members of the governing board of MSAN, an organization of inner-ring suburban school districts devoted to the purpose of eliminating achievement gaps (we discuss MSAN in detail in chapter 1). All of the superintendents of MSAN districts constitute the governing board, but we sought to interview those who had been in their current positions and had been members of the governing board for at least two years. We decided two years was probably a good minimum yardstick to apply to ensure that we were talking with leaders with enough experience to shed light on the questions we wished to pose. We wanted to talk with those who had a long-time commitment to closing achievement gaps, and some of these superintendents' efforts had started well before the term *achievement gap* was coined and before NCLB was even on the horizon. As it turned out, all but one of the fourteen superintendents who met these criteria agreed to be interviewed.

Our study addressed how these superintendents became involved in tackling achievement gaps, their understanding of what causes these gaps, how they chose to respond to the equity challenges they faced, and their assessment of their progress and success. Although we focused on the superintendents, we recognized that they operated in specific contexts and worked with critical allies in long-term efforts to close achievement gaps. Our analyses of superintendents and the organizational environments of their school districts helped us to conceptualize how the improvement of minority student achievement occurs.

In addition to the superintendents' experiences in working to diminish achievement gaps, we believed the school districts they served would provide prime examples of how these gaps might be attacked. Most of the districts served small to mid-sized diverse student populations, were well resourced, and were situated in inner-ring suburban communities. Their size suggested they might be more nimble in responding to gap-closing needs than larger organizations, but large enough to staff gap-closing initiatives. Their resources, moreover, suggested they would be better positioned than cash-strapped organizations to finance their efforts. Finally, their diversity suggested they might represent more realistic tests of gap-closing strategies than districts that served either largely white students or students of color.

Most of the superintendents whose experiences provide the core of this book were interviewed in the spring of 2011. Each was interviewed for a minimum of one hour. Face-to-face interviews were conducted with ten of them. Of these interviews, four were conducted by both of us and six by only one of us. All but two interviews were conducted during a MSAN governing board meeting that was held in Arlington, Virginia, over a three-day period. The interviews occurred in a hotel or in a high school. Three telephone interviews were conducted by one author during the same period. The two remaining in-person interviews were conducted later in the fall of 2011 and in late summer of 2012 in the offices of the superintendents of Alexandria and Arlington, Virginia, respectively. We recorded all interviews.

Before we began the interviewing process, we developed a protocol based on concepts articulated in *Gaining on the Gap*.[5] We were flexible about the order in which we asked particular questions based on the flow of the discussion, finding often that interviewees would answer some of our questions before they were posed. We attempted to create a comfortable discussion rather than a formal interview. Across all of the super-intendent interviews, we managed to ask or discover:

- How they worked on achievement gaps became a priority in their district
- How they personally became involved in working on achievement gaps and what in their personal history might have animated them to do so
- The role played by the school board, the community, or other actors in making closing gaps a priority and in maintaining that priority
- How they defined the achievement gap and explained it to faculty, staff, parents, and the general community
- Their goals in relation to the gaps
- The ways in which progress was achieved, measured, and communicated
- Programmatic and organizational initiatives they directed toward narrowing gaps
- Barriers, challenges, or threats they faced; the sources of these barriers or challenges; and how and the degree to which the obstacles were overcome
- The initiatives and accomplishments of which they were proud and the mistakes, if any, they made along the way

After transcribing the interviews, we sent the transcripts back to the interviewees and asked them to correct any errors and to add any clarifying comments they thought appropriate and helpful. Only three provided corrections or additions. We then read the transcripts multiple times to discern basic themes and develop the conceptual framework with assistance from concepts articulated in *Gaining on the Gap* and the literature of organizational learning.[6] In addition to generating the conceptual framework, the process of repeated reading and discussion of the transcripts yielded themes for each chapter of this book and provided the basis for data coding. In summary, we used a constant comparative method to identify unique characteristics of each superintendent's leadership on the achievement gap issue and searched for commonalities that emerged across the group's experiences.[7]

The method we employed is intended to consolidate and organize the knowledge these superintendents derived from their leadership experiences. We do not propose to generalize to all school districts and leaders, but we believe there is much to be gained from understanding how these superintendents in comparatively well-resourced inner-ring suburban school districts were able to make progress in mitigating or eliminating a variety of achievement gaps that militate against educational equity. It is our intent that educators generalize from their own contexts to these cases, finding alignment with their own experiences and learning from others.[8]

WHY WE WROTE THIS BOOK

While the thirteen interviews are the foundation of this book, it goes beyond reporting what we found by integrating the superintendents' words with relevant literature and our own experiences. We seek a larger audience because we became convinced that these superintendents were doing important work and, in the main, were doing it very well. Their examples, we believed, could be digested and adapted by many other school districts across the country whose student bodies are growing increasingly diverse and that are concerned about implementing strategies that will create conditions of equity. We imagine superintendents, school boards, communities, teachers, and other leaders borrowing the ideas contained here and adapting them to their own educational contexts to accelerate progress in closing achievement gaps. We have two purposes in mind for this book beyond describing and explaining the superintendents' work: (1) to illuminate what equity-focused superintendents have been able to achieve in their school districts, and (2) to synthesize their experiences, along with previously published organizational theory and research, into a model or conceptual framework that informs the work of narrowing achievement gaps going forward. Collecting superintendents' experiences into a reasonably coherent system helps others to generalize to these specific cases. Thus, we aspire to go beyond exemplary cases from which readers can easily turn away by claiming their situations are different to suggest a lens that can be used to look at any situation and find promising means for narrowing achievement gaps.

Investigating superintendents' perceptions in particular, as we do here with a relatively large number of participants, brings to light conditions conducive to addressing achievement gaps, specific strategies and tactics applied to serve underperforming minority students, and reflections on many years of work in this area. As we wrote the book, moreover, we wanted to maintain these superintendents' voices because we believed their experiences, behaviors, and motivations are best described by them and because they had important stories to tell. For this reason, we employ a large number of direct and sometimes extended quotations. We anticipate these quotations, as opposed to our characterizations, will more likely enable readers to capture the flavor of the superintendents' perspectives and appreciate the work in which they engaged.

In the academic realm, we move beyond declaring the existence and extent of achievement gaps to explain how the leaders we interviewed address them and why they have made some of their critical choices. Our empirical findings and theoretical development can serve as a guide to future research aimed at articulating influences on successful and struggling attempts to give all students socially just educational opportunities. In practical terms, this book adds to our knowledge of what superintendents, schools, and school districts should consider doing to make progress on this important national priority.

THE LARGER MEANING

Learning and publishing the thought processes of social justice–minded superintendents is important to understanding and, ultimately, being able to implement means of improving the life chances of this nation's most challenged students. Instead of trying to determine if we should tear down the country's school systems, we are more interested in figuring out how to make what we have work better. Doing so is vital because even the most desperately needy schools, no matter how low performing, are anchors in their communities. When they close, trauma and dislocation follow. Charter schools and independent schools of various types show some promise of narrowing achievement gaps, but the charter model is not universally successful. The worst charter examples perform less well than traditional public schools; charters at best display the kind of variation that exists within the traditional K–12 system.[9] With the vast majority of the nation's school-age children attending traditional public schools, the various manifestations of achievement gaps represent an educational problem in urgent need of attention.

The thirteen superintendents represented in this book are frank about the struggles they have experienced, but they are also a source of hope and optimism. Their strenuous, practical efforts point the way for others, not in terms of "best practices," but as examples of where to focus energy and attention and how to think about the root causes of the persistence of achievement gaps. We in no way intend to convey the notion that these superintendents, individually or collectively, have "fixed" the achievement gap problem, but they have made progress. Understanding the nature of that progress from personal recollections and through an analytical lens is of great importance to learning how to improve educational equity within public schools.

SEEKING EDUCATIONAL EQUITY

Taking school systems as they are, with both their failures and successes, the primary question in front of superintendents who participated in this study is: *What can we do to change the educational experiences of previously underserved students such that they learn and perform at a level close or equal to those who have traditionally thrived in the US education system?* From a more academic perspective, we ask: *What will it take to get to a point where student achievement is no longer reliably predicted by characteristics such as race, poverty, second language, and disability?*

The challenges are relatively simple to state, but potential solutions are complex. After decades of striving for equity, perhaps beginning with the *Brown* decision in 1954, we have learned the hard way that pet solutions alone—a little more money for economically disadvantaged, choosing English immersion over bilingual education, or response to intervention—have minimal impact on achievement gaps. The conceptual problem is that children are not outputs that respond to one or two or three specific inputs. They are human beings who exist in and are influenced by systems—schools, school districts, their families, their neighborhoods, and society. The superintendents whose wisdom we draw on for this study all recognized that schools and the social systems in which they are embedded interact, and therefore, as leaders in their districts, they must look not only at their schools and districts systemically, but also understand how the organizations for which they are responsible interact with systems over which they may exercise little or no influence.

A LOOK AHEAD

This book is organized to help the reader make sense of superintendents' efforts to close achievement gaps across their experiences in different contexts. We begin chapter 1 by describing the development and a bit of the history of MSAN. A brief profile of each of the thirteen superintendents follows, as well as their reflections on the progress they believed occurred during the time of their leadership. This first chapter also establishes context by addressing the similarities and differences of the MSAN member school districts led by the superintendents we interviewed. In chapter 2, we introduce the conceptual framework to orient the reader to our analytical perspective and to lay out the general challenges and opportunities embedded in persistent achievement gaps. Chapters 3–7 use the conceptual framework to analyze and interpret specific strategies and tactics employed by long-serving superintendents to close achievement gaps. By organizing the chapters according to superintendents' decisions and actions, we provide readers an inside perspective on the puzzles, dilemmas, and paradoxes of efforts to enhance social justice within public education.

To move their schools and districts into addressing long persistent achievement gaps, participating superintendents recognized the need to adopt a systemic perspective. Chapters 3 and 4 address two important organizational conditions necessary for success in this enterprise. Chapter 3 explores the idea that closing achievement gaps is not a matter of quick fixes; rather, it requires a considered, thoughtful, persistent, and sustained approach over a number of years under conditions of organizational and political stability. Chapter 4 examines how the levels of agreement or disagreement among members of the community, the board, and the superintendent regarding the priority of closing gaps are critical in predicting the degree of success a school district will enjoy in achieving that end.

Chapters 5–7 move from organizational conditions to a discussion of three strategic considerations. Chapter 5 demonstrates the degree to which superintendents agreed with Elmore's view that capacity for change must be created before improvement will occur and describes the ways in which different superintendents attended to the professional development of their faculties in the interest of building equity in their school systems.[10] We explain how their perspectives differed in working toward that end. Chapter 6 focuses on differences between participating superintendents as they describe opportunities they created for youngsters to narrow achievement gaps. In this chapter, we also grapple with the relationship between opportunity and achievement gaps and the potential of schools to address both. Chapter 7 uses Bolman and Deal's four frames model to analyze ways in which achievement gap work could be stalled or otherwise thwarted in the school districts these superintendents led and describes a variety of ways the superintendents countered such threats.[11]

Chapter 8 revisits the conceptual framework to identify the most powerful strategies and tactics employed by participating superintendents and to explain strengths and weaknesses in the framework itself that were revealed as we applied it to superintendents' experiences. We clarify lessons learned from the superintendents to suggest to both education professionals and education researchers fruitful paths ahead.

HOW TO USE THIS BOOK

We believe that superintendents, school administrators, teachers, school board members, other community members, and students of education leadership will find the portrayals of how various superintendents approached the goal of narrowing achievement and opportunity gaps to be deeply engaging. We hope that superintendents and other education leaders will find inspiration in the ideas and actions of those who have given their professional stories to this book.

Beyond aspiring to kindle resolve to create greater opportunities for students and narrow gaps in opportunity and achievement, we believe there is guidance in the conceptual framework, in the ways in which the superintendents approached their sets of issues in their organizations and communities, and in the lessons learned. At the same time, we recognize that specific initiatives must be determined by the context of individual school districts, schools, and communities. We expect that researchers will be able to make good use of the conceptual framework as they pick up the trail of discovering more widespread and nuanced results from teachers, site administrators, superintendents and their deputies, school boards, and community members striving to create more equitable, socially just outcomes in public education.

CHAPTER ONE

Superintendents of the Minority Student Achievement Network

Founded in 1999, the Minority Student Achievement Network (MSAN) began with fifteen superintendents committed to diminishing the power of race, ethnicity, income, and dominant language to predict student achievement. From the start, participating superintendents created a program of research and development that has affected the practice of school districts for the past sixteen years. MSAN was founded with the idea that school districts with shared interests and characteristics working together with university partners could fashion a research agenda directed at practices designed to resolve the most important, persistent, and challenging problem faced by schools in the United States.

To our knowledge, when it was founded, MSAN was the only organization of its kind. In subsequent years, other organizations of districts formed to combat the persistence of achievement gaps, but typically their memberships comprised districts of different sizes or more regionally based districts, or their work involved a much broader focus that may have included closing achievement gaps as only one of many priorities. This chapter introduces MSAN, describes the superintendents whose work constitutes the focus of this book, and summarizes selected examples of their accomplishments in narrowing gaps.

THE FOUNDING OF MSAN

In February 1999, Allan Alson, while superintendent of the Evanston (Illinois) Township High School District 202, invited other superintendents from around the country to a meeting in conjunction with the American Association of School Administrators (AASA) national conference held in New Orleans. He reached out to those with whom he had worked and solicited the names of others from Paul Houston, then executive director of AASA. Alson was hoping to attract superintendents of diverse, small to medium-size, and well-resourced suburban inner-ring school systems who shared his interest in working through issues related to narrowing achievement gaps. The fourteen superintendents who attended the meeting (a fifteenth had been unable to attend but would later participate in the formation of MSAN) led school districts meeting that description, both demographically and in size—student populations ranged from a couple of thousand to about twenty-five thousand.[1] Only two members of that original group of superintendents were still in their school districts and interviewed in preparing this volume. They were Mark Freeman of Shaker Heights (Ohio) and Neil Pederson of the Chapel Hill-Carrboro City (North Carolina) school districts.

That initial discussion, facilitated by Robert Peterkin, a former superintendent and the leader of the Harvard Graduate School of Education's Urban Superintendents Program, forged a general agreement that they wished to work together on decreasing race- or ethnicity-linked achievement disparities and that their work on that issue would be enriched by collaborating with scholars around the country dedicated to the same end. The session ended with the superintendents' commitment to bring selected members of their staffs to a June 1999 conference to be held at Northwestern University in Evanston. The purpose of the conference was to explore the establishment of what became MSAN. It featured an address by education scholar and psychologist Edmund Gordon, who at the time was working with the College Board and co-chaired that organization's Task Force on Higher Minority Achievement.[2] Additionally, sessions were held outlining the work on narrowing gaps in which a number of districts were engaged and a few work sessions focused on the development of the organization itself.

THE ORGANIZATION OF MSAN

MSAN established its headquarters during the spring of 1999 in Evanston Township High School. After the June conference, the group began to take form, guided by the idea that working together with the help of committed scholars, these districts, all relatively well resourced, could exert a salutary impact on their respective achievement gaps. In July 1999, the Joyce Foundation awarded a grant to the College Board to help MSAN develop its plans for research. The fifteen superintendents, now called members of the governing board, met again in November 1999 in Nashville to further develop the organization's design and plan.

The initial MSAN districts included:

- Amherst-Pelham Regional Schools, Amherst, Massachusetts
- Ann Arbor Public Schools, Ann Arbor, Michigan
- Arlington Public Schools, Arlington, Virginia
- Berkeley Unified School District, Berkeley, California
- Cambridge Public Schools, Cambridge, Massachusetts
- Chapel Hill-Carrboro City Schools, Chapel Hill, North Carolina
- Cleveland Heights-University Heights School District, University Heights, Ohio
- Evanston-Skokie School District 65, Evanston, Illinois
- Evanston Township High School District 202, Evanston, Illinois
- Madison Metropolitan School District, Madison, Wisconsin
- Montclair School District, Montclair, New Jersey
- Oak Park Elementary School District 97, Oak Park, Illinois
- Oak Park and River Forest High School District 200, Oak Park, Illinois

- Shaker Heights City School District, Shaker Heights, Ohio
- White Plains Public Schools, White Plains, New York [3]

Along with MSAN's major purpose to discover, investigate, and implement principles and practices that might lessen the power of race and ethnicity to predict student learning, the founders believed that they should set a research agenda for the organization and then find scholars who shared their interests in addressing the agenda. To advance the research mission, Gordon assembled a group of academics who became the Research Advisory Board. The Board included an impressive group of scholars committed to the goals of MSAN, including Wade Boykin (Howard University), Jomills Braddock (University of Miami), Anthony Bryk (University of Chicago), Ronald Ferguson (Harvard University), Virginia Gonzalez (University of Cincinnati), Gloria Ladson-Billings (University of Wisconsin-Madison), Pedro Noguera (Harvard University), Meredith Phillips (University of California, Los Angeles), Claude Steele (Stanford University), Sam Stringfield (Johns Hopkins University), and Ronald Taylor (Temple University).[4]

The initial plan for research was based on the assessment that:

> A significant problem in dealing effectively with the achievement gap issue is the profound disconnect that exists between research and practice. The Network proposes a new model where action research is combined with scholarly research. Practice will be used to inform research and research in turn will be used to affect practice. This will be accomplished through a collaborative practitioner-researcher model where research will be collaboratively designed, conducted, analyzed and published. It is expected that every district will have an internal process, which includes teachers, students, parents and administrators providing input into ideas for Network research and activities.[5]

The Research Advisory Board came together formally only twice, once in New York City in March 2000 and again in a meeting at a work session during the April 2000 annual American Educational Research Association meeting held in New Orleans.[6] It is not altogether clear why the Board did not continue as a part of the MSAN operation, but we suspect it had much to do with the very different reward systems of higher education and in school districts; that is, tenure-track professors are expected to publish results in peer-reviewed journals and typically have well-developed research agendas that may not necessarily fit the research agenda of school leaders.[7] The fact that the superintendents wanted to set the research agenda in accordance with their priorities for school improvement rather than adopt current research priorities of the individual scholars may have also been a deterrent for some members of the Research Advisory Board.

The Research Agenda and Scholar Allies

Although the formal advisory group never met again, a few of those scholars, and many others whose research interests or personal commitments coincided with MSAN priorities, became involved in a variety of initiatives across the MSAN districts. That group included Ron Ferguson, Gloria Ladson-Billings, Pedro Noguera, Wade Boykin, Sam Stringfield, Uri Treisman (University of Texas, Austin), Susanne Donovan (Strategic Education Research Partnership [SERP]), and Adam Gamoran (University of Wisconsin-Madison).

In 2000, Ferguson conducted what he called a "youth culture survey" of forty thousand grades 6–12 youngsters across all of the MSAN districts; the first major collaborative research of the group. The survey was used to discover what students of different ethnicities were experiencing in schools that might be contributing to achievement gaps. The superintendents made this their first joint effort because it was seen as a helpful way to derive a better understanding of achievement gaps, and the project met with general agreement to participate from all of the districts: a good way to start a collaborative effort. Most of the items were drawn from the Ed-Excel Assessment of Secondary School Student Culture developed by John Bishop of Cornell University. In addition, Ferguson included five items contributed by MSAN.

Laura Cooper, who was the assistant superintendent of Evanston Township High School District at the time and a prime thought leader of the Research-Practitioner Council (see below), reported that the planning, development, and analysis of the results of the survey helped the organization develop its identity and research agenda, and assisted it to better understand ". . . what students of different racial and ethnic groups were experiencing in school that might be affecting their achievement."[8]

Smith recalls conversations in which members of the Arlington staff, as well as superintendents from other MSAN districts, anticipated great differences in responses from the students across the districts, based on their perceptions of the unique composition and quality of each school system. As it turned out, very few differences by district emerged. A few major conclusions that cut across all of the districts helped to advance MSAN's work. Citing a 2002 report authored by Ferguson, Cooper summarized some of those findings:

> . . . (a) compared to White students, African American and Latino students reported lower grade-point averages, less understanding of teachers' lessons, and less comprehension of assigned reading; (b) as a group, White students reported greater socioeconomic advantages than African American and Latino students; (c) when asked about the reasons for working really hard in school, African American and Latino students were more likely to emphasize teacher encouragement and less likely to identify teacher demands than White students; and (d) although White students are more likely to complete homework assignments, students in all groups value doing well in school and, in fact, spend about the same amount of time studying, even though African American and Latino students turn in homework less frequently.[9]

Ferguson helped interpret the survey results in meetings with the Research-Practitioner Council and in meetings with individual school district staffs. Three of these findings engendered particular interest across the network because they belied conventional wisdom and framed problems that might be solved on the school district, school, or teacher level:

- The finding that among the forty thousand students responding, African American or Latino were as likely or more likely than white students to encourage their peers to do well in school. This finding contravenes the generally accepted belief that negative perceptions of "acting white" among students of color caused those students to intentionally avoid doing well in school. In fact, in a few of the districts, the group least likely to support academic effort among their friends was white males.

• Similarly, the belief that African American and Latino students worked less hard on assignments and homework was contradicted by the finding that African American and Latino students were just as likely as white students to spend time on homework, although less likely to turn it in.

• Finally, the finding that African American and Latino students were more likely than white students to respond positively to teacher encouragement and less likely than white students to respond positively to teacher demands provided a variety of suggestions of strategies for encouraging these youngsters.

In addition to conducting youth culture surveys, Ferguson led workshops in a number of districts to help interpret survey results, discuss ways in which schools could use the results to help diminish gaps, and to explain his Tripod model.[10] Ferguson also made frequent presentations at MSAN conferences, including student conferences, where he explained the achievement gap and helped students formulate plans to reduce it, implemented his Tripod project and made parent education presentations in many of the school districts. Gloria Ladson-Billings, in addition to conducting workshops on instruction likely to attenuate achievement gaps and presentations about this during MSAN conferences, including student conferences, made presentations in many MSAN school districts on instruction likely to narrow achievement gaps and on what she called the "education debt" as opposed to "achievement gaps." She also served for one-year as the interim executive director of MSAN when the organization's offices moved from Evanston to Madison, Wisconsin, in 2007. Like Ladson-Billings and Ferguson, Pedro Noguera made a number of presentations about the causes of achievement gaps, leadership to focus on reducing them, and ways to lessen them through instruction at MSAN functions when he was a professor and school board member in Berkeley, California, and in his later positions. Boykin also spoke at MSAN conferences and in a few MSAN districts about gaps but focused less on gaps than the development of talents of all students. He also worked with a parent group in Arlington to help them formulate what they might do to narrow achievement gaps Stringfield consulted with Alson and others on the development of a relational database that would allow comparisons of student achievement to be made across MSAN districts despite the differences in state assessment systems, although that particular initiative never came to fruition.

For a number of years, the MSAN annual meeting was conducted at a different host school district each year. The meeting lasted for two to three days. Each district would bring a team of five or more administrators, teachers, and sometimes school board members to the meeting, which usually included addresses by scholars and experts secured by the host school district, as well as presentations on practice by selected school district representatives.

Shortly before MSAN moved its headquarters to Madison, Gamoran, a professor of sociology at the University of Wisconsin-Madison and the executive director of the Wisconsin Education Research Center (WECR), was one of a number of UW-Madison faculty members who participated in MSAN governing board pre-meetings. These sessions, held the evening before governing board business meetings, were added because the superintendents wanted to make certain that along with the discussion of organizational concerns, they could devote time to discourse on current research surrounding issues of minority student achievement. In these informal, yet clearly focused sessions, Gamoran and other scholars who participated shared their research related to MSAN's priorities.

Treisman and Donovan were involved in a project designed to increase the enrollment of students of color in Algebra 1 across several of the MSAN districts. Treisman brought to the project what he had learned in earlier studies and from additional studies conducted in the participating MSAN districts regarding increasing minority student achievement in mathematics. The algebra project followed the SERP model, where school district representatives identified the problem and SERP then identified scholars across the country who might help with solving the problem and helped find resources to fund activities directed at solving the problem and evaluating the effectiveness of the solution.

This process mirrored the original intent of the Research Advisory Council and helped alleviate the earlier disappointment felt by some of the superintendents that the Research Advisory Board initiative had never jelled. SERP's similar role, combined with the participation of individual scholars, helped superintendents understand and resolve problems of practice and greatly benefited the research agenda of the MSAN Research-Practitioner Council.

The Research-Practitioner Council

In addition to working with academics, governing board members turned their attention to involving members of their staffs in the organization. MSAN's organizational plan of 2000 called for the establishment of a Research-Practitioner Council, whose mission it would be to plan and execute the organization's research and development agenda.[11] The Council was made up of staff chosen by the superintendents; each superintendent appointed one or two people, often including an assistant superintendent. Council members were in charge of research, minority achievement, and instruction or some combination of the three. The organizational plan also included a set of variables for understanding and improving the achievement of students of color, including:

- Teacher expectations

- School structure

- Curricular design

- Instructional delivery

- Teacher training

- Assessment practices

- Early childhood literacy

- Parent involvement

- Peer pressure/youth culture[12]

Although all of these variables continued to be of interest, over the course of subsequent meetings, the Council decided that research should focus on mathematics, literacy (with an emphasis on adolescent literacy), student-teacher relationships, and conversations about race and achievement. These areas of focus were approved by the governing board a few years later, and remain the current priority issues of MSAN research.

MSAN Services and Value

To accomplish its agenda, MSAN secured grants, promoted research by collaborating scholars (e.g., the research initiatives by Ferguson, Treisman, and others mentioned above), sponsored and conducted institutes for teachers and administrators, reached out to school boards of the various districts, and conducted an annual student conference.

First held in the second year of MSAN's existence, the student conference was designed to bring together high-achieving students of color from across the districts to discuss overcoming barriers to achievement and develop plans to increase the involvement of students of color in challenging academic experiences. Typically, the conference also included activities in which student representatives from each district would interact with scholars, including Ferguson, Ladson-Billings, and Noguera. In most cases, the students would return to their districts and report on their experiences and their plans to the superintendent and the school board.

The student conferences were organized and hosted each year by a volunteer school district. The district administration, typically with participation of an advisory group of district students and with the assistance of MSAN staff, would plan the conference. The student conference organization model mimicked the original organization of the MSAN annual conference, with a different host school district each year.

MSAN superintendents seemed to see the annual student conference as one of the greatest contributions of MSAN to the participating school districts. Bill Lupini, Jim Lee, Betty Feser, and Judy Wilson all spoke positively about the impact of the annual student conference, Most of the superintendents also mentioned the student conference as a benefit of MSAN membership and related stories of how the follow-up on those conferences had resulted in student-led work, particularly on encouraging other students of color to participate in rigorous academic experiences. Bill Lee provided an example of the impact of the conference in the Paradise Valley district:

> After the student conference, our kids came back . . . and they created a buddy program in their high schools for minority kids who take AP and honors classes. They have buddies to encourage them and mentor them and coach them . . . in an effort to increase our numbers. It's a pretty positive thing.

Summing up the importance of the student conference for the Princeton Public Schools, Judy Wilson said:

> One of the huge pillars of MSAN for me . . . is the student conference. While it's about professional learning for lots of people in our district every year and getting the opportunity to be in small, mini-institutes around narrow slices of subject matter, that's great for my faculty and my administrators, but the student conference is just unparalleled . . . I think it has the potential to be life-altering for those kids who get that kind of experience . . .

The host district administration, typically with participation of an advisory group of district students and with the assistance of MSAN staff, would plan the student conference.

Along with the student conferences, the MSAN plan had suggested that school board members be invited to participate at the annual conference, but this initiative had mixed results. Mark Freeman described how the conversation about including school board members in the annual conference changed, depending on what was happening to superintendents across the school districts. When school board–superintendent relations were generally positive, school board members were more likely to be involved. However, when relations became strained, the inclusion of school board members was questioned. For example, in 2002, when it was announced that Saul Yanofsky, the highly respected superintendent of the White Plains, New York, school district would not have his contract renewed after over twelve years in the position, a number of superintendents soured on the idea of having school board members attend that year's annual conference.

Nevertheless, the annual conferences did typically include school board members from many of the districts, and at one point a separate strand of sessions was created and planned for the conferences by school board member representatives. These sessions turned into what were termed School Board Assemblies, which were planned by selected school board members and facilitating superintendents across the districts. The assemblies remain among the activities of the MSAN organization. The annual conferences, however, were discontinued when the 2008 recession constrained budgets and travel became more difficult to support.

In the first few years of the MSAN's operation, there were also teacher conferences hosted by volunteer school districts in which university scholars and school district teacher leaders participated. In a few cases, the issues of minority student achievement were combined with teacher-as-researcher activities. As in the case of the annual conferences, and for the same reasons, the teacher conferences were discontinued after 2008.

The institutes, or mini-conferences, hosted by individual districts, nevertheless, continue. Held two or three times per year, they are focused more narrowly on a particular achievement gap problem or intervention, such as measures to take to decrease the disproportionate representation of students of color in special education. The MSAN Institute, held in Madison, now appears to substitute for the annual conference. For example, the 2013 MSAN Institute included a presentation by Smith called "Superintendent Decision Making and Achievement Gaps," which summarized the interviews on which this volume is based.[13] The 2015 MSAN Institute held in late April was devoted to "the latest research and promising practices regarding how school districts develop equity-focused leadership and ensure cultural competence," particularly as they relate to English language learners. The keynote address, *"It's Like Opening Pandora's Box: Lessons Learned from Families of ELLs,"* was delivered by Lorena Mancilla a specialist working in the Wisconsin Education Research Center on WIDA (World-class Instructional Design and Assessment) standards. The other major presenter was Ladson-Billings. A student panel discussing student development and a number of breakout sessions devoted to issues of ELL development fleshed out the agenda of the institute.[14]

MSAN TODAY

MSAN has changed since its inception in 1999. For the first eight years, its headquarters was centered at Evanston High School and the staff work of the organization was directed largely by Allan Alson. He and members of his staff were instrumental in forging the first relations with university scholars and securing foundation support for the organization's activities. After the adoption of the organizational plan in 2000, moves were made to secure resources and create a staff in addition to the administrators in Evanston. One of the governing board members, Rossi Ray-Taylor, superintendent of the Ann Arbor school system, left that position and became the executive director of MSAN. The same year, John Diamond (an assistant professor at Northwestern at the time, currently a faculty member at the University of Wisconsin-Madison and a continuing resource for MSAN) became the part-time director of research for MSAN.

In 2007, to relieve the Evanston staff of administrative responsibilities, a decision was made to move the offices of MSAN to a university. The governing board settled on the University of Wisconsin-Madison's Wisconsin Center for Educational Research (WCER) as MSAN's new home. The WCER was selected because it was known to be one of the largest education research centers in the country; its faculty and staff included many nationally recognized scholars; and the Madison Metropolitan School District and its superintendent, Art Rainwater, were original MSAN members. In the first year that the office was established at WCER, Gloria Ladson-Billings, already a friend of MSAN, served as the interim executive director until Madeline Hafner, the current executive director, was appointed after a national search. In joining MSAN, Hafner was returning to the University of Wisconsin, where she had earned her PhD seven years before.

In addition to calling for the development of a staff, the organizational plan prescribed the expansion of the number of member districts by a couple of districts a year, up to twenty-five. The number of MSAN districts grew from fifteen to twenty-five by 2004. As of this writing, there are twenty-eight member districts, ranging in size from about seventeen hundred to thirty-four thousand students. Twelve of the districts are founding members (only Berkeley, Montclair, and White Plains departed); the sixteen that later joined are:

- Alexandria City Public Schools, Alexandria, Virginia
- Birmingham Public Schools, Birmingham, Michigan
- Brookline Public Schools, Brookline, Massachusetts
- Buckeye Elementary School District #33, Buckeye, Arizona
- East Lansing Public Schools, East Lansing, Michigan
- Farmington Public Schools, Farmington, Michigan
- Federal Way Public Schools, Federal Way, Washington
- Greenwich Public Schools, Greenwich, Connecticut
- Harrisonburg City Public Schools, Harrisonburg, Virginia
- Issac Elementary School District 5, Phoenix, Arizona
- Middleton-Cross Plains Area School District, Middleton, Wisconsin
- Paradise Valley Unified School District, Phoenix, Arizona
- Princeton Public Schools, Princeton, New Jersey
- School District of South Orange and Maplewood, South Orange, New Jersey
- Sun Prairie Area School District, Sun Prairie, Wisconsin
- Verona Area School District, Verona, Wisconsin

Typically, school district departures from membership coincided with changes in superintendents. The fact that only two of the original superintendents remained when we conducted our interviews (and those two have since retired), yet twelve of the initial fifteen districts retained their membership, suggests that the succeeding superintendents and/or school boards found value in the organization. This conclusion is reinforced by our study. The superintendents we interviewed clearly believed that MSAN represents a valued and appreciated support for their work on closing achievement and opportunity gaps. They were excited by and committed to the research conducted by cooperating scholars and their own staffs that helped to inform their practices that would make a difference for youngsters long underserved in their systems. MSAN research helped them understand root causes of achievement gaps. In addition, the superintendents valued the activities of the institutes, mini-conferences, and the student conference as ways of assisting their staffs and students to address the issues of equity and opportunity gaps.

A sense of support also derived from the camaraderie provided by the governing board, a forum in which superintendents share concerns, speak frankly without fear of public inspection of their thoughts or opinions, and generally serve as good colleagues to one another. When the board was first established, it set explicit and understood conventions that governed its interactions. One early agreement was that only superintendents would attend the governing board meetings, with the exception of the two assistant superintendents who were leading the Research-Practitioner Council (from Evanston Township High School and Shaker Heights); in other words, superintendents would not delegate attendance at the board meetings to subordinates. Second, it was understood that opinions expressed in the meetings would remain confidential. Thus, each of the superintendents was free to express opinions, provide support for those opinions, or try out new ideas. These understandings led to discussions that were valued by many of the superintendents, who found the sharing of views helpful to making progress in their individual districts.

THIRTEEN SUPERINTENDENTS STRIVING FOR EQUITY

We now turn to a brief description of the superintendents we interviewed for our study, including how each came to adopt narrowing achievement gaps as a priority in his or her school district; their personal history in relation to social justice; a thumbnail sketch of their districts (these are described in greater detail in appendixes A and B); the number of years served in their districts (at the time of the interviews, they were all serving in MSAN districts); information on their experience both inside and outside MSAN districts (detailed in appendix C); and a few of their self-perceived accomplishments in diminishing opportunity and achievement gaps during the time they led their school districts. Among the thirteen superintendents, one is African American (Hardy Murphy) and twelve are white, three are women (Elizabeth Feser, Susan Zurvalec, and Judy Wilson) and ten are men.

Elizabeth Feser—Windsor Public Schools (Connecticut), 2002–2011

Located in suburban Hartford, Connecticut, the approximately thirty-six hundred– student Windsor Public Schools had the second-highest proportion of minority students of the thirteen districts represented by our superintendents—70 percent. Betty Feser noted that it also had one of the highest concentrations of black professionals of any school district in the state, yet achievement gaps persisted. As we discuss in more detail in chapter 3, Feser had a difficult time getting her board focused on addressing achievement gaps because of disagreements about how to define them. Nevertheless, she led the district with quiet persistence driven by her sense of personal mission.

Windsor was her only superintendency in nearly forty years of work in education. When asked about her motivation, Feser recalled the racial tension that informed her early experiences as an educator:

> My first experience . . . was in parochial education in Boston, and was in an urban school in the South End during the time of busing. [T]hat was my first experience . . . really working in a school where the minority was the majority. But secondly, the whole issue of race, poverty, and in the period of busing when white flight was rampant and people were fleeing to parochial education, we were a school of 85 percent black and Latino students . . . [T]hat was my first experience, and I was really drawn to it. When I moved into public education, [I found I had] a calling to a degree with urban—I guess, if you want to use the term, *downtrodden*—or the less fortunate kind of kids, so that's part of it.

In discussing progress demonstrated in narrowing gaps, Feser mentioned, among other things, that she had data indicating that the percentage of students of color attending four-year colleges had dramatically increased; she cited in particular the rise in their acceptance at the University of Connecticut. She also referenced the narrowing of proficiency gaps on the state tests and greater participation of students of color in the math leagues, where they had previously been altogether absent. Along with a couple of other superintendents, she pointed to the movement to provide full-day kindergarten, which has been associated with gains in the achievement of students of color and students of lower-income families. As did many other superintendents, Feser pointed to the increasing number of students of color in AP classes as the sign of a shrinking opportunity gap.

When we interviewed Feser, she had recently been recruited for and accepted the position of superintendent in Milford Public Schools (Connecticut) (not an MSAN district), where she earned the distinction of Connecticut Superintendent of the Year in 2015.

Mark Freeman—Shaker Heights Schools (Ohio), 1988–2013

The longest-serving of our thirteen superintendents, Freeman spent nearly his entire K–12 public education career in this district. Embedded in a planned community that was started by wealthy Cleveland businessmen in the early twentieth century as a homogenous enclave, Shaker Heights eventually embraced ethnic and racial integration despite the intent of its founders. Although most of our superintendents intentionally climbed an administrative ladder into their superintendencies, Freeman describes his experience as a somewhat indifferent student who worked his way into teaching, became interested in diversity issues as they gained ascendancy in the school district, and gradually shifted into administration when called to do so.

In his interview, Freeman did not dwell long on himself, preferring to focus on core issues and describe what others had achieved during his tenure as superintendent. During the brief portion of his interview when he spoke directly to the question of his own motivation for social justice work, Freeman explained:

> I began to look at [bias] and kind of study it. I suppose in a very, very personal standpoint . . . I always . . . had an interest in prejudice or bias, whether it's my own, which I have, or somebody else's and why it occurs. [In the 1960s and 1970s] it was a fascinating place to look at this. So, in one sense I guess I

embraced it. But it was thrust upon me and . . . I never thought there was any other way to go. I mean . . . I don't want to overdo this. I guess I just assumed it wasn't morally right . . . I don't think I thought of it as a choice. Well of course, you would do this.

Freeman also indicated that while progress was difficult and halting over a number of years, Shaker Heights did succeed in diminishing the opportunity gap by increasing the proportion of African American young-sters in advanced classes. He also picked up a professional development theme common among the superintendents when he recounted how teachers in the district, initially reluctant to support more open oppor-tunity in advanced classes, now take pride in the progress the district has made and in their role in encouraging and supporting students in taking advantage of the opportunity to be challenged at higher levels.

Serving twenty-five years as superintendent in a challenging district of approximately fifty-four hundred students, almost equally divided be-tween black and white, is a testament to Freeman's leadership skills and ability to work productively with school board members and the broader community. He retired in 2013 and currently serves as the executive in residence at Cleveland State University.

Jere Hochman—Bedford Central School District (New York), 2008–2015

The combination of a 1960s-era commitment to justice and a teaching career as a social studies teacher shaped Jere Hochman's dedication to providing more equitable education for all students. In the trenches of the St. Louis voluntary desegregation plan as a teacher, principal, and ultimately superintendent, Hochman learned a great deal about bringing disparate groups that did not know each other together for productive ed-ucational experiences. Hochman traces his development as a professional committed to social justice in the following way:

I really kind of saw the value of [education] and I would say that simultane-ously, growing up in the sixties . . . being a Midwestern observer of the civil rights movement going on, and being inspired by that is probably where I became really focused on the work of leveling of the playing field for kids of all races, even in terms of the student exchange when I was in high school and, you know, visiting schools in the city. I grew up in the typical, non-integrated suburbs. So it started for me very young in terms of who I am . . . [I]t became very real in terms of policy, probably . . . by my seventh or eighth year of teaching, when our school district in St. Louis became part of the St. Louis voluntary desegregation plan. And [I was] teaching out in the predominantly white suburbs in a huge school district of twenty-some thousand kids at that time . . . the response to the very first bus that rolls up from the city of St. Louis with African-American kids on it [was overwhelmingly negative]. Fast forward to when I became superintendent of that same district, [where] I was the chairperson of the voluntary desegregation plan . . . At its peak, we had over thirteen thousand African American kids voluntarily going out to one of eighteen county school districts . . . It was my day job then to make sure that that was going to work, and to be outspoken about the fact that it was our responsibility to make it work out in the predominantly . . . white suburbs . . . [We] began to put achievement data out in front of people before folks were actually looking at achievement data and looking at other issues related to race and equity at that time.

Hochman moved on from Missouri to become the superintendent of the Amherst-Pelham Regional School District (Massachusetts), where he served from 2003 to 2008. An original MSAN district, Amherst-Pelham was already committed to narrowing achievement gaps and working toward social justice. The move to Bedford returned Hochman to his suburban roots to some extent, but the district encompasses separate towns that are different racially and socioeconomically. The approximately forty-five hundred–student Bedford district has the largest proportion of white students (65 percent) and the highest per-pupil expenditure of the school systems represented in this book, with diversity expressed in the quarter of the students who are Latino. As in many districts, children come from largely segregated communities into integrated schools that are striving to generate harmonious social relations among members of the schools' student bodies while narrowing achievement gaps. Hochman described focusing the system's attention on equity issues and making the discussion more prominent while promoting action to make progress.

Hochman pointed to progress in narrowing the performance differences of students of color and white students on the New York state tests and was proud that it was occurring more quickly in Bedford than in the rest of the state. However, he noted, as did a few superintendents in other states, that some of the progress had been stymied when the state tests were recalibrated. He also reported that the representation of students of color in advanced classes had improved during his time as superintendent. (In late October 2015, New York's governor Andrew Cuomo announced Hochman's appointment as the state's Deputy Secretary of Education.[15])

James Lee—Paradise Valley Unified School District (Arizona), 2009–Present

Jim Lee, the current president of MSAN, was one of three superintendents among those participating in this study who had moved from an assistant superintendent position to superintendent of the same school district. Unlike in many of the other interviews, we did not elicit Lee's personal motivation and perspective on issues of race and social justice. Lee preferred to focus his telephone interview on the equity work he led in his district rather than on his personal story. His over-thirty-thousand-student district is the largest in the organization. His discussion of gap-closing programs he helped implement in Paradise Valley revealed both the pride he felt in the progress the district was making—particularly with students whose first language is Spanish—and the frustration of trying desperately to meet students' wide range of needs in a district and state strangled by a lack of resources.

As discussed in later chapters, Lee did his best to leverage Title I money to provide programs and staffing for the children in his district with the greatest need. With federal money, Lee estimated his total per-pupil expenditure at $5,000, far below any other MSAN district. The Arizona School Boards Association reports that Arizona's per pupil expenditure has declined 24 percent since 2008—from $4,654 to $3,529, the lowest in the nation.[16] Just before our interview, Lee had spoken to a state legislator about allocating more revenue to education, but had met with defensiveness and unresponsiveness. Lee was energetic and willing to fight for equity. But despite reporting considerable progress, he was doubtful about closing achievement gaps in the absence of a major infusion of resources to allow additional interventions and extended time to learn.

William Lupini—Brookline Public Schools (Massachusetts), 2004–2015

Brookline is the third superintendency over a twenty-year span for Bill Lupini, who previously worked in the role in Kutztown, Pennsylvania, and Beverly, Massachusetts. A former president of MSAN. Lupini revealed his passion and determination to meet the needs of underserved students when discussing his relations with the board and community and implementation of various interventions intended to narrow achievement gaps. He pointed to hiring more administrators and teachers who shared backgrounds with students of color as an accomplishment of his tenure. What made him most proud, however, was shifting the conversation in the community:

> I'm particularly proud that there's an open conversation about this right now. That seems small, doesn't it? But there's actually an open conversation about these issues in our district now. Many people have said to me, "We were looking at the achievement gap fifteen years ago." And maybe they were . . . But I think there was an awful lot of *looking* at the achievement profile—"Let's not lift up the hood." There was certainly no putting it out in [the open]. I mean, the first Our Schools [a public relations document issued by the school district describing the Brookline schools] in Brookline was published for realtors to use . . . [The realtors] probably [love it] because it does lay out all those things about our schools and say this is a place . . . that looks at what it is they do. They're willing to be honest and say this is a good district and we can get better.

Lupini believed that things *were*, in fact, getting better. In addition to seeing greater proportions of students of color in advanced classes, Lupini described a ten-year concerted effort of summer and afterschool interventions directed at students living in a couple of public housing projects, which were designed to support learning and prevent regression. He indicated that before the interventions, about 20 percent of these students went to college after leaving Brookline, compared with 80 percent for the entire Brookline student body. In the year of the interview, 90 percent of the public housing students entered college. The district had also implemented a calculus project that was creating an increase in the proportion of students of color engaged in upper-level mathematics classes.

After having been selected Massachusetts Superintendent of the Year for 2015, Lupini departed Brookline in the fall of 2015 to become the interim superintendent of the Essex Technical High School in Danvers, Massachusetts.[17]

Hardy Murphy—Evanston-Skokie Community Consolidated Schools District 65 (Illinois), 1999–2012

Typical of most of the superintendents we interviewed, Hardy Murphy viewed his efforts to narrow achievement gaps as integral to his entire career in education. When asked how he came to be so public about working on achievement gaps, Murphy replied,

> I think it's always been part of my mission as a public educator . . . [P]rior to assuming the superintendency, I had been involved in work [with] the achievement gap throughout my career, ranging from the days when I was the [desegregation] monitor in the district prior to . . . coming to Evanston. So, yeah, it has always been just a part of . . . being an African American. It was something that has been kind of a driving force in all of my endeavors in public education.

Murphy focused on racial equity during his career and was also passionate about providing greater equity to special education students. He found race and special education linked because black students were disproportionately identified for special education services.

As superintendent of the over seven-thousand-student Evanston-Skokie elementary/middle school district, Murphy focused heavily on changing teacher and principal expectations for achievement among African American and Latino youngsters and revising instructional processes for all students. He attributed the decade of growth in the proportion of African American students meeting mathematics and reading standards from about 30 percent to 85 percent (close to the same proportion as white students) to changes in both instruction and expectations.

Following his thirteen-year tenure in Evanston, Murphy has worked in the position of research scientist/scholar in the Indiana Institute on Disability and Community at Indiana University in Bloomington. His work on behalf of disabled students continues there; he also focuses on teacher and principal evaluation.[18]

Patrick Murphy—Arlington Public Schools (Virginia), 2007–Present

After nineteen years as a teacher and administrator in neighboring Fairfax County (Virginia) Public Schools (interrupted by a relatively brief stint in Frederick County (Virginia), as an assistant superintendent), culminating in the role of assistant superintendent for accountability, Pat Murphy succeeded Smith as Arlington's superintendent. Mindful of the district's achievement during the previous twelve years, Murphy picked up the achievement gap-closing theme as highly valued by the board and the community:

> I think it should be pointed out that the district has done a lot of work over the past decade to get itself to where I came on board. It did a number of things to specifically focus on eliminating the achievement gap. That work was done by the previous superintendent. It was also done by several previous boards as they have moved on . . . It is really wrapped around the values that the community has about this as one of its main priorities. I think it is important to have that as a context. I do look at this as a continuum as far as us moving forward as we continue to narrow the gap.

Murphy noted that the Arlington school system, with a student population of over twenty thousand, experienced considerable progress in narrowing pass rate gaps on state tests. For example, across all of the grades and subjects tested by the state over more than a decade, the pass rates of African American students increased by 108 percent, cutting the gap as compared with white students by 57 percent; and the pass rates of Latino students increased by 79 percent, reducing the gap with white students by two-thirds. He also pointed out the increasing representation of African American and Latino students in AP and International Baccalaureate (IB) classes, while the district maintained a high proportion of qualifying scores on the AP and IB tests.

Murphy, the Virginia Superintendent of the Year for 2015 and one of four finalists for National Superintendent of the Year, views himself as addressing opportunity globally. He is equally concerned about helping families understand how to finance college as he is about ensuring that all students have access to challenging course work and curricula. He continues the work on cultural responsiveness and opening doors for students in the widely diverse Arlington community.

Daniel Nerad—Madison Metropolitan School District (Wisconsin), 2008–2012

Dan Nerad's career as a superintendent spans fourteen years and three school districts. After a long career in other positions in Wisconsin's Green Bay Area Public School District, he served as superintendent for seven years, then assumed the role of superintendent of the Madison district (over twenty-five thousand students) for four years, and is currently superintendent for the Birmingham (Michigan) Public Schools. Green Bay and Madison were MSAN districts under Nerad's leadership (Green Bay has since left the network), and he has continued his commitment to MSAN by recently bringing the Birmingham Public Schools into the organization.

Nerad expressed vigorous determination to close achievement gaps:

I personally feel [disparate performance by race among students is] our number-one social justice issue in this country . . . We know that there is nothing in the biological sciences that would predict [a] relationship between race and achievement. But we know that one exists today. I think if we are truly about creating bright futures for all kids, it has to be about elevating performance for kids who are furthest away from meeting standards. It has to be done in a way that allows them the full range of educational programming and options that are available in school today . . . We have to think about this in counterintuitive ways . . . [W]e have to be about accelerating instruction for kids that are furthest away from meeting the standards. We have to find ways that we can allow these kids to experience our most rigorous course work, knowing that they may not be prepared for that course work today . . . it's about opening up those doors. It's about recognizing that relationship [between race and achievement] exists today, but doing all the things we can through quality instruction, to make it different.

In addition to a major push for professional development and improving instructional practices, Nerad took particular pride in working with community members to ameliorate the disparity in out-of-school factors and early education that many scholars believe widen race- and income-related academic performance disparities. He worked with health-care partners to find health services and/or insurance for over two thousand children who would not otherwise have been covered through state insurance. Through community collaboration, the Madison Public Schools also established nearly universal access to education among four-year-olds. The district was able to enroll fourteen hundred of eighteen hundred eligible children, mostly children of color, in what Nerad called "four-year old kindergarten."

Brian Osborne—The District of South Orange and Maplewood (New Jersey), 2007–2014

In the fourth year of his first superintendency at the time our interview, Brian Osborne offered the most detailed reasons of all the superintendents for making closing achievement gaps the signature effort of his superintendency. He spoke with the passion of a political radical about why he made this his life's work. As a recent college graduate greatly influenced by time spent in Latin America, Osborne went into teaching armed with his fluency in Spanish to reach a student population he perceived to be victims of a corrupt system:

> My thinking at the time was, here we have communities that are in our country and in our schools because of what I considered at the time a very evil imperialist US policy [reference to refugees from the civil war in El Salvador and US support of the Contras in Nicaragua]. And to sort of complete the circle of evil, when their kids get to our schools, they're considered stupid for not knowing English.

Teaching elementary school in impoverished neighborhoods in New York City, Osborne was fueled by his own white middle-class upbringing in suburban Oak Park outside of Chicago, a community committed to integrated housing before fair housing was legislated. (Oak Park's elementary and high school districts are also MSAN members.) Immigrant children in New York experienced no such integration and support a generation later. Optimistic about what could be done to help children catch up to their peers, yet frustrated that the gains didn't seem to last, Osborne became an intern under Harvard's Urban Superintendents Program and began his apprenticeship in central office administration. Upper-echelon administrative work in the New York City Department of Education provided him with experience he took into his initial superintendency.

Reluctant at first to put his name in for the South Orange and Maplewood District because it wasn't the kind of urban setting for which he hungered, Osborne soon learned about the challenges of inner-ring suburban school districts typical of MSAN members. Osborne expressed gratification about working in the well-resourced district of sixty-five hundred students. Although the district was diverse (no majority group, 39 percent African American, 49 percent white at the time of the interview), when Osborne arrived, it had experienced separation of students by race, by expectations, and by accompanying levels of curriculum and class assignments that had generated decades-old achievement gaps.

Osborne characterized the implementation of full-day kindergarten as a triumph for the work on opportunity gaps. At the other end of the K–12 spectrum, he was encouraging more African American students to go to college and conducting follow-up studies that initially indicated a huge gap between the proportion of students of color and white students who after five years had graduated from college (19 percent and 50 percent, respectively). Three years later, the number of students of color who graduated was proportionally larger, although the gap remained wide. Osborne attributed the change to the district's work to elevate access and quality of instruction K–12.

After seven years in South Orange and Maplewood (2014), Osborne moved on to become superintendent in the City School District of New Rochelle (New York).

Neil Pederson—Chapel Hill-Carrboro City Schools (North Carolina), 1992–2011

The other of the two original members (with Mark Freeman) still in his school district when interviewed for this volume, Neil Pederson became familiar with the diverse (52 percent white, 15 percent Asian, 14 percent Latino, and 11 percent African American), nearly twelve-thousand-student Chapel Hill-Carrboro City district during his five years as assistant superintendent. He served under Gerry House, the first female African American superintendent in the district, and spoke admiringly of the way she led the organization. He credits her with beginning to look at disaggregated data that revealed achievement gaps for African American students under the more positive veneer of high average test scores. When she left to become superintendent in Memphis, Pederson was appointed to replace her and picked up the achievement gap theme as ". . . the most intractable problem that the district had. It was unacceptable. I think it was pretty unanimously unacceptable throughout the community, and I indicated that it was what I would focus on more than anything else."

Pederson spoke of his motivation for addressing achievement gaps in terms of ethical imperatives:

> I went into education largely out of a desire to make society better . . . I was probably mainly motivated to go into education because of growing up or being in college during the civil rights movement and other types of social unrest. I saw this as sort of a moral calling.

One of the leaders in MSAN's work on cultural competence for faculty and staff, Pederson described considerable improvement in narrowing proficiency rate gaps on state tests for African American students. When the district adopted its focus on the gap, about 30–40 percent (depending on subject and grade) of African American students were proficient, compared with 80–90 percent of white students. Before the state standards changed in 2005, proficiency rates had risen to nearly 100 percent for whites and Asians and to around 82 percent for African American and Latino students. He recounted similar, but less dramatic, progress in the representation of African American and Latino students in advanced classes and in graduation rates.

In the last of his nineteen years as superintendent in Chapel Hill-Carrboro at the time of his interview, Pederson reflected that community support for equity work remained strong throughout, and he characterized his superintendency as relatively harmonious. Given the length of his tenure, this was not surprising. Since 2011, Pederson has served as executive director of the Central Carolina Regional Education Service Alliance.

Morton Sherman—Alexandria City School District (Virginia), 2008–2013

It was unusual for the superintendents we interviewed to be confrontational. The impression we got from Mort Sherman, however, is that in his district he could be downright pugnacious in confronting racism directly and publicly. He served in several superintendencies before arriving in Alexandria, including eight years in the Cherry Hill Public Schools (New Jersey). (Cherry Hill was an MSAN district under Sherman's leadership, but is no longer.) The 12,400-student Alexandria district, with the smallest proportion of white students (28 percent) and the largest proportion of Latino students (30 percent) of the districts represented in this book, remains in MSAN two years after his departure.

During his five years leading the Alexandria district, Sherman tended to focus on changes in those schools that were largely African American and Latino and had been performing poorly in relation to state and national standards. He described one elementary school with an 8 percent white enrollment, for instance, that had received a great deal of attention through his instructional initiatives and reached a 98 percent pass rate on the state mathematics test. He was also proud of the changes he attributed to instructional initiatives at T.C. Williams, the district's one high school, which had been identified by the state and federal governments as a "persistently low achieving school." After infusion of considerable federal money that funded multiple Sherman initiatives, it officially shed that label and was being celebrated as a success story.

Sherman's controversial approach generated both devoted followers (the school board chief among them) and strong detractors. He left the school district in 2013 after an election that put seven new members on the nine member school board. He now serves as associate executive director of AASA, The School Superintendents Association, the national superintendents' organization where, among other things, he coordinates the work of a collaborative organization of school superintendents.

Judith Wilson—Princeton Regional Schools (New Jersey), 2005–2013

During her career of more than thirty years in public education, Judy Wilson devoted at least two-thirds of that time to working in school districts that had a high proportion of minority students. Her first superintendency was in Woodbury, New Jersey (not an MSAN district), with a student population that was 50 percent white and 50 percent black. Wilson was adamant that she wanted to work only in a place that would address diversity and equity issues directly and vigorously:

> [I]t's just who I am, what I've been about, and how I was raised. Some of it, I think, is at the core of who I am as a person . . . [I]t's really all mission-driven, that's what it is . . . And I would not go to another district—after my first 10 years I specifically would not locate in another district unless it were already truly committed to the issues of equity. I had no interest in any of the districts that were not dealing openly with these issues and with that set of goals. So, it's just been a part of my life for a very long time.

Wilson perceived herself as working closely and cooperatively with the Princeton community to maximize educational opportunities for all students in the thirty-five-hundred-student school district. Among other initiatives, she focused on pre-K services for four-year-old children who would otherwise not be receiving early education instruction. Over a four-year period, the district provided the services half time, but service was extended to full days in the following three years for all of the children. Citing progress in more proportionate enrollment of students of color in advanced high school classes and of those taking university classes while in high school, she nevertheless believed the district had a long way to go before it could claim any real success on those initiatives. Wilson's energy and commitment were palpable throughout our conversation. She retired in 2013 and at the time of this writing was working as an independent consultant.

Susan Zurvalec—Farmington Public Schools (Michigan), 2005–2014

Like Neil Pederson and Jim Lee, Sue Zurvalec served as an assistant superintendent in her district before becoming superintendent. She arrived in

Farmington near the end of more than a decade of shifting demographics as more black families exited Detroit for the suburbs in search of better education and prosperity. When she became superintendent fifteen years later, the district had been an MSAN member for two years, and socially just educational outcomes were of paramount concern. Zurvalec understood that many black parents who represented over a quarter of the approximately 11,500 students district at that time were disillusioned by persistent achievement gaps.

Along with most of the other MSAN superintendents, Zurvalec provided specific examples of progress in addressing the opportunity gap in advanced course enrollment. The district had eliminated prerequisites for AP classes and encouraged students of color to enroll, and over a three-year period the enrollment of African American students tripled (total enrollment doubled). There was no corresponding decrease in the proportion of students earning qualifying scores on the advanced placement tests.

Zurvalec worked with community agencies, the community at large, and black parent leaders to mitigate fear and suspicion regarding the intent and motivations of the school district leadership so that all could engage in problem solving more effectively. Her equity work was infused with a strong sense of personal mission, fueled by high energy and enthusiasm, much like many of the other participating superintendents. She retired in 2014 and currently works as a human resources coach and executive consultant.

As we completed our interviews of the superintendents, it became clear that all of them could support their contention that their districts had registered progress in creating opportunities and diminishing gaps in achievement. Although expressing it differently, they also shared a strong commitment to ensuring socially just results from their work in education and a resolve to thrust that priority forward. Similarly, while they approached their work in different ways, all strived to create conditions leading to increased opportunities and decreased achievement gaps through organizational learning, the focus of chapter 2.

CHAPTER TWO

A Framework for Equity

Solving problems in education can be understood through the lens of organizational learning—the proposition that meaningful and lasting change occurs when organizational performance gaps are deeply understood and addressed by changing constraints imposed by the status quo.[1] Organizational learning in schools and districts is guided by the direction leaders establish and the vision they articulate.[2] The conceptual framework presented in this chapter captures how the superintendents profiled in this book thought about and took action to enhance the learning of previously underserved students in ways that narrowed achievement gaps. It therefore serves as a key analytical tool for understanding what the superintendents envisioned, what they were doing, and how they did it. We begin with a discussion of organizational learning as it relates to pursuing equity and then draw from superintendent interviews to explain how organizational learning worked for them in practice. Figure 2.1 is a graphic representation of the conceptual framework we describe in detail with the help of examples.

ORGANIZATIONAL LEARNING TO NARROW OPPORTUNITY AND ACHIEVEMENT GAPS

Learning in educational contexts is most naturally focused on students. We wish to shift that focus to the adults inside schools and districts as organizations in the belief that when adult learning takes place, then

FIGURE 2.1   Conceptual framework for pursuing educational equity
in a school district

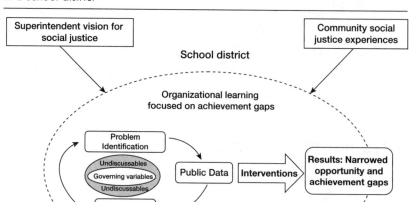

changed behavior in the classroom becomes possible.[3] Learning and resulting action can be stymied when organizational factors protect the status quo, but organizational learning is a means to challenge current practice and to improve individual and system performance. In the context of
achievement gaps, organizational learning is the means by which schools
and districts discover how to narrow them. We draw from the original
theorists and applications of organizational learning to clarify how we apply these concepts in education contexts.

Organizational learning begins with understanding the difference between aspirations and outcomes. In the climate of NCLB, the difference
between what majority populations achieve and what other segments of
the student population (such as those in poverty, racial and ethnic mi-
norities, English language learners, and students with disabilities) are able
to accomplish represents a stark gap between aspirations and outcomes

that is fundamentally important to the future of non-majority students. Argyris and Schön, the source of much of our thinking on organizational learning, distinguish between what they call *espoused theories*—what we *say* we believe—and *theories in use*—what we actually *do*. For purposes of developing the conceptual framework we use in this book, we use the terms *aspirations* (what we say we want), *actions* (what we do), and *outcomes* (type of change) because they are more accessible and more clearly describe what is happening as educators draw conclusions about student achievement data. When actions are taken that alter implicit and explicit rules and align outcomes with aspirations, Argyris and Schön call the result *double-loop learning*.[4]

One of the remarkable achievements of NCLB is the way in which it has focused schools and districts on the difference between aspirations and outcomes with respect to student achievement. The law has taken sporadic state attempts to test for achievement of standards and made more universal the use of generated data to drive school- and district-level decision making. Minority student achievement as compared with the majority of the student population is no longer masked by reported averages. At the same time, social justice issues have taken center stage based on the belief that educational outcomes matter for students' ultimate life chances. The college preparatory nature of state standards elevates college matriculation and persistence as clear symbols of educational equity and success.

Obvious though it may seem that schools and districts would address the gap between aspirations and outcomes, the gap must first be *perceived*. Argyris and Schön employ the device of *undiscussables*—in simple terms, those topics we choose not to talk about—to explain why critical perceptions may not happen. However, there are powerful reasons to avoid discussing problems. The status quo, Argyris and Schön claim, protects individuals and organizations in important ways that center on competence.[5] Problems that aren't discussed can't be changed and therefore the status quo remains. If as principal or teacher I acknowledge that achievement gaps exist in my school, then I may perceive myself as culpable—I am not serving the cause of social justice because I perpetuate inequities. Individuals shield their vulnerability by avoiding discussion and acknowledgment of the gap between aspirations and outcomes. At the system level, this manifests as a predisposition to reflexively emulate solutions that other schools and districts have adopted to address the problem. DiMaggio and Powell explain that the inclination for organizations to resemble one another—isomorphism—in the same field or institution is driven by the pursuit of legitimacy, which further protects the individual.[6] The natural tendency to avoid culpability and pursue legitimacy generates an unwillingness to open up undiscussables regarding achievement gaps. Thus teachers, principals, schools, and districts protect the status quo and come under fire from those who claim that the system is broken.

Yet achievement gaps are undeniable for many districts, which often grab for quick fixes. Such responses may lead schools and districts to adopt "best practices" (for example, from websites such as the US Department of Education's What Works Clearinghouse). The district's legitimacy is assured by addressing achievement gaps through influential, research-based approaches to common teaching and learning problems in mathematics and English language arts. Adoption of routines streamlines decision making and helps the organization to change in marginal ways that may pay off in terms of achievement growth. But it reinforces isomorphic tendencies.

Argyris and Schön argue that altering routines in response to a problem without addressing undiscussables will lead to what they term *single-loop learning*.[7] The changed behaviors that result from this type of learning are immediate responses to a problem's symptoms, but do not address its cause. The lack of substantive organizational change means that the unaddressed causes eventually lead to the resurfacing of the original problem—an endless cycle. For example, consider the effect on the achievement gap by the adoption of an elementary school reading program. The program itself may adequately address specific reading problems that have surfaced through data analysis, but there may also be underlying social-emotional and socioeconomic issues that have a meaningful impact on minority student achievement. The result is likely to be that the reading program yields gains in achievement for all students, but the gap between minority and majority students remains.

The MSAN superintendents were unusual because of their willingness to name and address undiscussables they believed were impeding progress on achievement gaps in their districts. This behavior was pivotal for them, as we explain in detail in chapter 3. Making undiscussables discussable enables organizations to engage in *double-loop learning* that leads to substantive change through questioning and changing policies, values, and assumptions that led to the original problem.[8] An example from one of our superintendents shows how this works. Betty Feser was experiencing resistance from the Windsor Public Schools board on the issue of comparing African American students' test scores to those of white students. She was surprised that this resistance was coming from some of the black members of the board. As she probed deeper, she found that the constant comparison became pejorative for African American students because they could never be recognized for improvements they were making as long as these data neglected to show how they were achieving at a higher level than many black students from around the state. By opening up this issue that had never been a part of normal district discussion, Feser was able to strike a compromise on data reporting to the public that consolidated board support for the efforts to close achievement gaps that she wanted to be the focus of her district leadership.

Addressing reported outcomes that had previously been undiscussable allowed Feser to shift focus away from arguing about what was perceived as inappropriate for one group of students toward changes the district needed to make to improve the achievement of those students who were performing at a level below the district as a whole and who were not meeting state standards. In Argyris's terms, she was poised to change *governing variables*—the explicit and implicit rules by which organization members function—thus achieving double-loop learning for the district.[9] Governing variables, if left unchanged, cement the status quo in place. In Feser's case, although she didn't put it in these terms, black community members were questioning the governing variable that white student achievement was the required standard. This particular governing variable is pervasive, rarely questioned, protected by numerous undiscussables, and enshrined in NCLB implementation. Change governing variables and the leader changes what people do and what is possible within the organization.

In another example, Farmington's Sue Zurvalec addressed the governing variable of curricular autonomy within schools. Before she began her change efforts, elementary schools in her district were left alone to determine what would be taught and by when. Although this autonomy would ostensibly allow teachers and principals to meet the unique needs of their student populations, Zurvalec hypothesized that this was actually one of the root causes of Farmington's black-white achievement gap because it was denying educational opportunities for some, probably in the name of meeting students' needs. For example, students of color were more likely to be denied entry into advanced classes or placed in "lower groups" within classes because of concerns based on prior teacher recommendations and/or on diagnostic measures of questionable validity that they might be "set up for failure." These "lower" groups or classes would not be exposed to the same knowledge expected of other students. Zurvalec's response was to change the rules by unifying the elementary curriculum across the district to ensure that all students were achieving the district's academic goals, particularly in literacy.

Organizational learning can be slow and difficult to engineer. Zurvalec and others describe the curriculum unification process as taking years. Yet many of the superintendents described organizational learning strategies as an important tool for shifting the status quo in their districts, though, again, they likely did not define their efforts in this way. Organizational learning as embodied by district efforts to change assumptions and the status quo is at the heart of systemic efforts to close achievement gaps.

The thirteen superintendents used data as a means to open up undiscussables in their districts and begin the process of double-loop learning. They did more than discover gaps through data collection and analysis; they made the data public, which had the effect of mobilizing their schools and community behind the effort to close achievement gaps.[10] Publicizing achievement gap evidence risked backlash, but doing so was a means to generate support for these superintendents' visions for student achievement and system improvement. After making the evidence public, the superintendents turned their attention from vision to action in the specific steps they took to employ organizational learning to improve instruction for underserved students.

GAP-CLOSING LEVERS

The concept of organizational learning is central to the conceptual framework and becomes more concrete when applied to superintendents' efforts to narrow achievement gaps. In the sections that follow, we employ the conceptual framework by explaining some of the specific steps the superintendents took to make changes in their districts in a manner consistent with organizational learning. These examples preview much of what we explain in depth in later chapters. We want to emphasize that not all of the superintendents engaged in the following practices all the time; this is a compilation of the efforts that led ultimately to specific interventions (see figure 2.1).

Vision

Establishing a vision for the school district is one of the core practices essential to leadership that influences student achievement.[11] Without a clear vision and sense of direction, schools and districts are more prone to maintaining status quo behaviors and achievement gaps remain unaddressed. But it is also crucial to ask where the vision is focused. The visions of these thirteen superintendents ultimately centered on the theme of social justice.

All of the superintendents espoused a vision for greater equity in student outcomes. They saw themselves as engineers of a more socially just school system that would correct at least some of the inequalities that existed in their school districts and surrounding communities. They understood, however, that for their vision to be achieved, others needed to be devoted to it as well. Consequently, the superintendents put a great deal of energy into working with their boards, district and school leadership, teachers, parents, and community members to build commitment to a vision for more socially just education. In figure 2.1, we place various constituencies and influences around the organizational learning process to convey the multidimensional nature of each school district's context.

As one would expect, the superintendents were not universally successful in achieving their visions, nor did those who experienced success always have a smooth ride in their effort to implement them. Nevertheless, they were clear about the directions in which they wanted to steer their school districts and what was to be achieved in terms of student outcomes.

These superintendents worked at the pleasure and served as the agents of the governing boards of their school districts. Although alignment between superintendents' and board members' visions was not always perfect (as we have seen in Betty Feser's case), every superintendent explained that a vision held in common with the school board was essential for their gap-closing work, and most expressed gratitude toward their board members who understood and wholeheartedly supported their work. They generally believed that their school boards were as committed to social justice and educational equity as they were. A strong working relationship with their school boards provided them with a firm foundation from which to change how their districts addressed achievement gaps. Indeed, if such alignment eroded substantially, superintendents knew it was time for them to seek a professional change.

Governing Variables

The MSAN superintendents questioned the written and unwritten rules in their districts that held an inequitable status quo in place. In organizational learning terms, they sought to install governing variables that would support social justice goals. The four governing variables that were most commonly put into place were:

- High expectations for all students
- High-quality instruction
- Access for all to rigorous teaching and learning
- Parental and community involvement

These served as reference points in their districts so that when anyone might wonder, "Why are we doing this?" superintendents could answer easily.

During the NCLB era—and for some participating superintendents long before—high expectations for all students became a mantra. Superintendents constantly reminded their schools and the community at large that all children deserved the opportunity to attain the highest levels of academic achievement. Some expressed this as having all students college-ready by the time they graduated from high school. At the same time, the superintendents were realistic enough to know that it was up to them to operationalize what they meant by maintaining high expectations. They worked with teachers, students, and parents to bring the day-to-day life of schools and classrooms in line with all students achieving at a high level. Closing the achievement gap in this area was especially difficult; superintendents typically found that outcomes were often out of line with explicit aspirations because the status quo simply didn't support high expectations for minority students.

High-quality instruction, which we define as including both the quality of the teaching and the quality of the relationship between teachers and students, follows naturally from high expectations, but can be equally difficult to realize. As part of this process, the superintendents pushed for improved instructional practices. They also preached higher academic standards for all students, inculcating the value of academic challenge within their schools. But they recognized that just pushing students harder is not an effective strategy. Thus, they emphasized the need to address affective challenges students faced, from poverty to institutionalized racism. In sum, they worked toward high-quality instruction by striving to be as comprehensive as possible in meeting students' needs.

Schools commonly establish competitive filters that serve, intentionally or not, to keep minority students away from opportunities for the most rigorous teaching and learning. Such filters undermine the effort to ensure high-quality instruction for all, because non-honors curricula tend to focus more on low-level learning of facts and algorithms rather than synthesis, analysis, and complex problem solving. At the high school level, the general pattern was for superintendents to take off the filters and allow open access to honors and AP courses. They understood, however, that minority students, who under the status quo would not be admitted to such courses, would require additional support to get into and thrive in the most academically challenging classrooms. The need to have all students ready for challenging work accounted, in part, for the urgency with which the superintendents pushed for a common curriculum at the elementary level. If all students did not have the same learning experiences, some were more likely to arrive in middle school or high school without sufficient academic foundation to handle the rigorous curricula that open the doors to college admission.

As with high-quality instruction, equipping students to succeed in challenging curricula also requires addressing their affective needs. Mark Freeman in Shaker Heights, Neil Pederson in Chapel Hill-Carrboro City, and Pat Murphy in Arlington are three examples of superintendents who recognized the need for cultural competence in teachers and culturally responsive teaching in classrooms, including the development of high-quality personal relationships between teachers and students. They provided teachers with ongoing professional development so that more classrooms would be safe and welcoming for a larger proportion of minority students. Such efforts are critical for persistence and success in classrooms with rigorous teaching and learning. The environment must be both challenging and nurturing.

A common theme for all of the superintendents was the need to communicate with and find support in the broader community. This imperative drove them to pull parents and other community members into the common effort to close achievement gaps. Parental involvement was given varying priority by the individual superintendents and took a variety of forms. Some were more traditional in their approach to parent meetings, while others pursued unusual incentives, such as providing language training at school during the school day to parents who spoke little English, to draw parents into the lives of their schools and, as a result, help them be more informed and involved in their children's education.

Problem Identification

Superintendents used the positional power granted by their school boards to install the four governing variables and thereby communicate the specifics of their social justice visions. They opened up discussion of a variety of achievement gaps and in so doing initiated processes of problem articulation. The central challenge for most was being stuck with long-standing achievement gaps and a certain degree of complacency about them. Taking steps to bring teachers, students, and parents face to face with a particular problem could all by itself create strong resistance. Hardy Murphy, in Evanston-Skokie, explained that ending the practice of special education pull-out for reading instruction in the elementary schools was important to him because it was largely the black and Latino students who were pulled out, and thus had curtailed access to the core curriculum. Teachers resisted because it added the complex task of differentiating reading instruction within a classroom with seven or eight more students in it. Parents of the remaining students resisted because they feared their children would not receive the reading instruction they needed. Murphy and other superintendents reflected that many of the systems accepted their visions at the conceptual level, but when confronted with specific problems requiring changed practices, they often feared moving away from what was comfortable and familiar.

Public Data

At times, superintendents tried to make changes before their stakeholders saw the need to do so. This led to battles that the superintendents did not expect and were not eager to fight. They found, however, that data provided grist for the critical conversations they wanted to have. By making data public, they were able to bring multiple constituencies to consensus regarding the problem(s) the district was facing, if not the specific solutions.

Publicizing data was a key means of surfacing undiscussables, which in turn would allow conversations about the extent and nature of the achievement gaps districts faced. But doing so can be seen as an attack, as demonstrated by the Feser example where black board members were opposed to the within-district comparisons between black and white students. The factor that pulled Feser out of that particular quicksand was that there was no denying that black student achievement was not meeting the expectations and aspirations of the community. Had Feser and the board's response to the internal disagreement been to avoid publicly focusing on the distance between aspirations and outcomes for black students, it might have been very much more difficult or impossible for her to pursue closing that gap in meaningful ways.

The superintendents all recognized that data would need to be disaggregated along multiple dimensions to shake community complacency with averages that looked strong relative to the states in which their districts were embedded. Now NCLB requires disaggregation, but superintendents such as Pederson and Freeman began the practice of examining subgroup achievement long before NCLB. They understood that they needed clear and compelling evidence of a problem in order to mobilize any sector of the community to address it.

Smith et al. use the case of the Arlington Public Schools to demonstrate that understanding the achievement picture in a school district requires far more than simple end-of-course exam data. During his twelve-year superintendency, Smith publicized data ranging from elementary grade reading levels to grade-level passing of Algebra 1 with a C or better to participation in AP courses. Furthermore, he and his colleagues publicized all of these data broken out by student categories such as poverty, second language, race, and disability.[12] Participating superintendents similarly found value in displaying student outcomes in multiple ways so that all of the district's constituencies could obtain a clearer understanding of how various students were progressing through the community's schools.

Data Analysis

The data in and of themselves do not explain very much. Organizing data into relevant categories is an important first step in analysis. Further interpretation of the data converts it into knowledge from which actions can be taken. Judy Wilson, Sue Zurvalec, Betty Feser, and Hardy Murphy recognized that their districts did not have a standardized curriculum within levels, which helped them to understand, at least in part, the differences that their student achievement data were revealing. They could then transform the achievement data into new knowledge that suggested leaving curricular decisions to the various schools was undermining efforts to achieve educational equity.

Data analysis was mentioned by all the superintendents as a central component of their effort to close achievement gaps, and when they publicized their data, they did so with interpretations that would help various constituencies understand the directions in which they aspired to lead their districts. Whether this meant purchasing instructional programs with Title I money in suburban Phoenix or exposing institutionalized racism in Alexandria, data analysis provided a critical means of explaining to school personnel and the community at large the problems these superintendents meant to address and their means for doing so.

CONTEXT

Superintendents were far from the only ones in their districts concerned about social justice. As previous examples illustrate, community members held strong opinions about what supported or thwarted equitable education outcomes. But the various communities affected superintendents differently, from those who felt a need to begin conversations about social justice to those who believed that they needed to steer a discussion that had started long before they entered the district.

The palpable desire for social justice within a district may be difficult to channel because of local and state conditions that reinforce inequities. State funding often results in widely varying per-pupil expenditures, depending on the relative wealth of districts. State test results are commonly interpreted in ways that do not acknowledge progress, a particularly acute problem when minority student achievement is beginning to rise. Housing patterns often keep communities segregated by race and socioeconomic status, and when students from these disparate communities come together in integrated schools, numerous challenges emerge. Educators do not control all of the inputs into the achievement gap problem. This lack of control is perhaps most starkly communicated by Jim Lee of the Paradise Valley Unified School District, on the edge of Phoenix. Lee reported that the per-pupil expenditures in Arizona ranked forty-ninth or fiftieth in the country. Most of the other districts we studied were spending at least twice to five times the amount he had available to educate his students. For Lee, the central problem was equity for students in poverty. It manifested as a high dropout rate triggered by low scores on state tests, particularly in English language arts. His only hope for channeling more resources to his students most in need was Title I, which he tried to maximize through promising programming.

Inequitable per-pupil expenditure is just one factor among many (e.g., poverty, poor postnatal care, absence of early childhood classes) that prevent less advantaged children from participating in experiences important to learning; what Carter and Welner and others have termed the *opportunity gap*.[13] These opportunity gaps, in turn, have a deleterious impact on learning and lead to achievement gaps. The predominantly inner-ring suburban districts represented here encountered many opportunity gap factors in their efforts to close achievement gaps. Examples range from labor market imperatives that kept parents working in multiple jobs to try to make ends meet to poverty that impacted child nutrition to a lack of social capital required to understand how to navigate the process of applying to and persisting in college. Such contextual factors are often ignored or used as explanations for the limitations of what schools and districts are able to accomplish with challenging student populations. The superintendents, however, were more likely to try to figure out how their schools and districts could reasonably respond to the opportunity gaps that existed in their communities so that the effects could be mitigated. For example, Dan Nerad in Madison found that students in poverty lacked health insurance; consequently, unattended health problems profoundly affected their learning. Nerad's conviction that students needed to be healthy to succeed in school led him to reach beyond direct educational services into the community to seek health care for his neediest students so that they would be ready to learn alongside their more financially secure peers.

INTERVENTIONS

Viewing our conceptual framework as a model that explains how one set of superintendents has approached closing achievement gaps, we go beyond the thoughts and choices—what might be considered inputs—to highlight the outcomes of superintendents' efforts. They put their plans into action through specific interventions based on implicit or explicit theories of action. A common challenge was to ensure that actions were taking place at the classroom and school levels that were consistent with gap-closing intentions. Different interventions were employed by different superintendents, from Osborne charging teacher collaborative teams in South Orange and Maplewood to engage in problem solving at the classroom level to almost all superintendents' insistence on professional development for teachers to give them greater capacity to address the needs of various minority student populations, and much more.

The interventions were where superintendents staked their claim to making a difference for students previously underserved by their school systems. They are specific gap-closing levers they pulled in their efforts to change the status quo. The interventions were intended to result in measurable evidence of gap closure, such as improvements in state assessments, upward trajectories in district benchmark assessments, participation rates in challenging course work, and improved dropout and graduation rates.

SUMMARY AND CONCLUSION

Participating superintendents employed organizational learning strategies to address the intractable problem of achievement gaps in ethnically and socioeconomically diverse school districts. Working within typical public school contexts that included multiple constituencies with varied interests, they fostered new ways of thinking about student achievement that required attention to two complementary organizational factors: undiscussables and governing variables. By making discussable the most important forces supporting an inequitable status quo, these superintendents were able to change governing variables and thereby move their school districts to enhance the education of all students. Evidence for change is found in results of the specific interventions superintendents implemented that were designed to narrow achievement gaps.

Narrowing achievement gaps is a process that is technical, social, and affective. The conceptual framework presented in this chapter captures the dynamics of how to address this central educational challenge of the early twenty-first century. By examining the specifics behind closing achievement gaps, we give education leaders and teachers access to helpful concepts for addressing the challenges in their own schools, districts, and classrooms. Moreover, we hypothesize a system—a set of dynamics—that allows leaders to think beyond single-loop learning quick fixes to engage in double-loop learning that changes the fundamental ways in which school districts do business. The conceptual framework also serves as an analytical lens for future research into achievement gap-closing efforts.

Progress toward achieving greater educational equity by addressing achievement gaps is episodic and uncertain. By clearly defining what they meant by various kinds of achievement gaps, the superintendents we interviewed for this book were able to put in place programs and processes that made a difference for students. They pointed to mitigating social inequities, improving test scores, increasing access to challenging curricula, full participation in the life of the school, and improved college matriculation as evidence of progress. Though not always easily measured, gap closing was palpable in all cases. How did they do it? We answer that question over the next five chapters, moving from macro to micro perspectives.

CHAPTER THREE

Ensuring Organizational Capacity, Stability, and Learning

Chapter 2 presented the conceptual framework we use to understand superintendents' efforts to mitigate or eliminate opportunity and achievement gaps. As we noted there, central to the framework is the concept of organizational learning, which helps explain efforts to achieve socially just education because it begins with comparing ideal to actual outcomes. In the case of opportunity and achievement gaps, this means comparing minority student achievement and opportunity to majority student achievement and opportunity, to state or other standards, or to some combination of the two.[1] But it means more, because many of the superintendents focused on how minority students engaged in the lives of their schools, measuring participation in challenging curricula, enrichment programs, and extracurricular activities. Every one of these conceptions of potential gaps asks two fundamental questions: (1) What do school district officials want all students to experience? and (2) Can students whose experiences are inadequate be identified by race, disability, poverty status, or first language? Answering these questions is the foundational work of addressing achievement gaps. At the beginning of their terms, the superintendents represented in this book found the answers to both to be unsatisfactory. Consequently, they worked with their school systems to make their organizational structures more robust, responsive, and stable as they endeavored to lead the larger school community on a learning path. When they were able to narrow achievement gaps in their districts, they did so in ways that were consistent with organizational learning.[2]

Taking an organizational—or systems—perspective on superintendents' work runs the risk of oversimplifying what they did and explaining their choices and pathways as more linear than perhaps they were, particularly because the qualitative data we gathered is all retrospective. Two challenges emerge. March warns against relying too heavily on retrospective accounts because of individuals' natural tendencies to filter and forget.[3] We add to March's point a belief that when asked, "What did you do about achievement gaps?" superintendents were likely, for the sake of verbal clarity, to place events in a more logical order than what might have actually happened. Second, in chapter 2, we presented examples of organizational learning in districts in a more linear fashion than they actually occurred. Applying organizational analysis to superintendents' recall and reflections helps us to understand choices superintendents made and resulting consequences, but the method can pull the discussion away from events as they occurred. In an effort to mitigate this limitation, we use numerous specific examples to explain organizational learning as it unfolded and explain trends for superintendents' actions rather than relying on one or two recollections.

ORGANIZATIONAL CAPACITY, STABILITY, AND CONTEXT

With the exception of Paradise Valley, MSAN districts are relatively well funded, with large variations across states and over time. A strong fiscal base is critical to organizational capacity. In good financial times, superintendents could provide more programs and training. But in 2011, in the wake of the Great Recession, they were more focused on how the loss of funds made their decisions more difficult. (We elaborate on the relationship between declining revenue and organizational stability later in this chapter.) Judy Wilson explained that Princeton was a place where resources were always available and how this helped her to enhance the quality of education for students typically underserved. But New Jersey's fiscal picture changed substantially after 2008, putting pressure on her initiatives. Though a few of the superintendents were buffered from the recession, most felt its effects and lamented how it limited the capacity of their school districts to provide vital gap-closing services.

Possibly more important to organizational capacity than financial resources is personnel. The insight and creativity of those working in the school district provide the fuel for innovative ideas and programs that make a difference for minority students. The personnel side of organizational capacity may be defined within the teacher corps as pedagogical content knowledge and among administrators as leadership. In nearly all cases, superintendents identified personnel decisions and professional development as their primary means for building the capacity of their school districts to close achievement gaps.

Strong school district organizations that have access to resources and skilled and motivated personnel are far more capable of organizational learning that leads to improvement of achievement gaps than those threatened by a lack of funding and/or shallow pools of expertise. Lee in Paradise Valley made this point when he proudly described programs that were changing how teachers taught and related to their students, then acknowledged he could only pay for them out of Title I money and therefore was not able to reach all of his district's schools. Brian Osborne and Judy Wilson feared the loss of personnel in the wake of New Jersey's fiscal retrenchment.

A less tangible, though no less important, aspect of organizational capacity is the motivation of personnel to address the needs of all students. Mort Sherman explained that teachers' will to address gaps was a bright spot in Alexandria (though he qualified this by adding that their will had to merge with skill to result in more effective teaching and learning). Many of the superintendents expressed their appreciation for teachers and administrators who were as passionate about achieving socially just educational outcomes as they were.

Also interwoven with school districts' organizational capacity is their stability, which both supports and is supported by adequate resources, skills, knowledge, and motivation. Nearly all of the superintendents came to districts that were experiencing some degree of organizational instability, which in turn diminished the districts' capacity to achieve goals. Hardy Murphy's perspective is typical:

> [T]he first thing we had to do was talk about developing plans and systems that all schools were responsible for implementing . . . [A]n alignment of this effort from the board and the central office through the schools and the individual classrooms was the first task at hand.

That their tenures lasted beyond five years is evidence that superintendents were able to stabilize their school districts at least to the extent that their contracts were renewed one or more times. Superintendents who served one district the longest (Mark Freeman—twenty-five years; Neil Pederson—nineteen years; Hardy Murphy—thirteen years; Bill Lupini—eleven years; and Sue Zurvalec—eleven years) recognized that they became important factors in the organizational context because they had been in place long enough to hire most of the leadership and teachers in their districts. Pederson, emphasizing motivation, explained that the opportunity to hire personnel over a long period of time helped to stabilize his school district and move it forward toward social justice:

> [A]s long as I've been there, it means that with the exception of one or two people, everybody [here], I've hired. [W]ith that comes greater loyalty. Hopefully, I've been successful in hiring people that . . . bring to us the beliefs that exist in our organization and are committed to the same goals. I've certainly seen a shift from in my earlier years having to deal with principals, in particular, who were not on board with this agenda, who retired or whom we encouraged to move on. So I think there's greater consistency across schools about the beliefs and practices that you find in the schools.

Community factors influence organizational stability at least as much as personnel. The location of MSAN districts in inner-ring suburbs means that their students represented a wide range of socioeconomic status. Superintendents emphasized the need to balance various parental and student interests across the school district. Achieving balance requires the organizational capacity to serve a wide range of student needs and the stability to implement and build programs. The task is made particularly challenging by the relative power and voice of the more affluent families. The superintendents understood that their social justice agenda would be strengthened if they were able to keep these families participating in the public schools. Doing so would help them maintain credibility, legitimacy, and financial resources. For many of the superintendents, this tension played out in the arena of gifted and talented programs and other advanced curricula, as it did for Dan Nerad:

> The message is, we need to improve learning for all kids, and advance achievement for all kids . . . while we eliminate these achievement gaps. And that's the more tailored message here . . . We've been in a lot of tension with our parents of talented and gifted kids here since I've come. Part of it is, they've looked at my coming as an opportunity to re-create a talented and gifted plan, which I've been more than willing enough to do. But they've also kind of used it in a way that is . . . continuously telling us we're not doing enough.

As mentioned, the budget plays a large role in determining the capacity of school districts to respond to achievement gaps, and budgets over time greatly affect stability. Thus, fiscal characteristics are an important contextual factor. By 2011, the federal stimulus response to the Great Recession had run its course. Most states and school districts were still reeling fiscally. Thus, in many cases, socioeconomic status tensions that existed before 2008 were heightened in the years that followed, making superintendents' political balancing acts even more difficult. Zurvalec's suburban Detroit district was hit particularly hard by the recession because of Michigan's fragile and declining economy—a general trend that had been in place for decades, punctuated by periods of relative prosperity:

> For many years we enjoyed affluence in Farmington. We had great resources. We could afford to fix a problem with money . . . [W]e could always add more people. The last couple of years in Michigan, the state budget crisis and the funding source, the way schools are funded in Michigan, has actually harmed the districts that were the best funded districts [more] than anybody else . . . Last year, when we had to restructure, when we closed schools because of declining enrollment . . . we had to be more efficient in our operations. What we have now is starting to emerge: a greater pushback from parents who started to worry that if your resources are being limited and you're putting more

resources into supporting kids who may be in need in terms of [academic support], or you're letting more kids go into AP classes and class sizes are rising, then how's my kid gonna be served? That is definitely out there now.

Pederson's perspective from a university town in North Carolina is similar:

> The way it typically comes out is that when times are tougher economically and we have to make decisions about what stays and goes in the budget, then you start having the gifted parents come out, the exceptional children's parents come out, African American parents come out and advocate for the constituency they represent . . . So when times get tough, the pushback is greater and until the past three years, times were basically not tough financially.

The main concern of superintendents during times of financial stress is that the work they had committed themselves to over long periods of time would be set back or ended.

A subtheme of guiding their districts through all the challenges of equalizing educational opportunities was figuring out an ethical and practical pace for change. Internal sources of stress that affect capacity and stability include actions the superintendent takes to make change. Superintendents who understand their districts' contexts face the uncertainty of how to pace their improvement efforts. For these thirteen superintendents, the main concern was moving forward while maintaining sufficient organizational stability so that they didn't become bogged down in crises. Freeman tended to take a gradual approach to addressing achievement gaps and was skeptical about leaders who showed up in districts wanting to make whirlwind changes to make their mark as reformers or in the name of what was right:

> How much turmoil can you have in the institution? That can also create a situation in leadership that's really negative . . . That doesn't mean you [don't] make changes and do lots of bold things . . . but somebody who always wants to tip everything over, say everything's bad, you know . . . they're going to fix it and they're going to leave. So, it's how far can you push it without [losing] the leadership and losing the stability of the district. I think that's very important in school districts that face a lot of the issues that MSAN districts do because we're talking in many of these districts about a community that's questioning, "How long [is] this place going to last? Is it going to fall apart?"

Yet some other superintendents expressed doubts about whether they had pushed hard enough early enough to make the kind of difference they intended. Betty Feser felt this about her own experience:

> The thing that I've wrestled with is, did I not move fast enough and hard enough? . . . I've always been concerned that if you push too hard, people retreat and dig in . . . You know, I moved cautiously. I made my message clear, but moved cautiously. And sometimes I wonder, was that a mistake? . . . [C]ould we have been further along if . . . I had pushed the agenda further, if I had taken the board on and just really confronted them . . . and said, "You've got to come together on this"?

Pederson also had second thoughts. He initiated difficult conversations in Chapel Hill-Carrboro, but after nineteen years, he wasn't certain that the conversations led to sufficient action:

> I think we've probably been spending too much of our energy and time on the conversation, not moving beyond the conversation. I don't think we want to skip the conversation, [but] it needs to have a greater impact than it has, in my opinion, on student outcomes. When I came to the district, our high schools were . . . integrated [but] the classes were very racially identifiable. I mentioned earlier [that] we took down some barriers, but they're still very racially identifiable. It still feels like we have schools of haves and have-nots.

Osborne was personally inclined to do more and do it faster, but he listened to the advice of others on his team who cautioned against hasty action:

> We've changed our approach to the so-called enrichment program in the elementary schools. We've changed some criteria and allow more kids to access the AP courses and high-level courses in the high school. I think incredibly modest steps. I mean, many people have talked me back, really, from what I think we should be doing, but the rationale [is] that every step we make has to be successful, because if we make mistakes, we're going to get slapped back hard or my tenure gets cut short, and who knows whether the next person will want to take on the work.

Mort Sherman's approach was practically the opposite of Feser, Pederson, and Osborne's. He believed that underlying vestiges of racism needed to be unambiguously exposed in order for the schools and the community to be able to address achievement gaps effectively. He knew that this was a difficult message for teachers and community leaders to hear, yet he made it a centerpiece of his superintendency. Courageous as Sherman may have been, his five-year tenure in Alexandria was the second-shortest among the thirteen superintendents.

In sum, the superintendents agreed that their districts required substantial capacity—horsepower—to make changes that would narrow gaps. Stability went hand in hand with organizational capacity, and they guarded stability carefully. In terms of the conceptual framework, superintendents attended to community experiences with and reactions to social justice efforts (the outer ring in figure 2.1) as they tried to maintain stability within their districts. Their own longevity in the role was key because the longer they stayed in a stable situation, the greater influence they had through personnel decisions, relationships with their boards, and trust in their communities.

Nevertheless, longevity alone was no guarantee that they could continue the work that was most important to them. Stability could be threatened if the school board turned over based on community discontent with the superintendent and/or the schools. Competing interests threatened harmony and consensus regarding some of their gap-closing efforts, and this threat was intensified when budgets declined. Navigating varied and shifting factors appears to have been a source of concern to most of the superintendents. There is no formula for addressing context effectively because it is ambiguous and difficult to understand in the moment, and it can change in unexpected ways. These superintendents stabilized their districts to the extent they could to maximize organizational capacity, allowing administrators, parents, and students to focus on the organizational learning necessary for continuous improvement.

DOUBLE-LOOP LEARNING IN CONTEXT

Simple as it sounds to compare a hoped-for outcome to an actual result—such as students with disabilities reading at a proficient level at the same rate as students without disabilities—examining the difference can be fraught with anxiety and defensiveness. The disability case may be among the clearest. If a student's disability involves difficulty processing written language, how can a fifth-grade teacher attend to this need while also meeting the needs of the non-disabled students in her classroom? Organizational learning suggests that this and other questions (for example, how can we teach mathematics to English language learners who understand mathematics, but not the English language?) can be addressed by first understanding the nature of the difference between aspirations and outcomes, then figuring out why that difference persists. Capacity to engage in this kind of exploration requires both an inquiry mind-set and processes to facilitate the search for answers. The superintendents worked hard to foster both.

An Inquiry Orientation

Jim Lee frequently turned to programs he could purchase with Title I money. One such was the Instructional Practices Inventory (IPI), an approach to peer observation and teacher collaboration designed to measure student engagement and increase higher-order thought.[4] Lee believed IPI could help teachers understand student engagement in their classrooms through a process of peer inquiry, analysis, and discussion:

> [T]eachers actually go in and observe fellow teachers' level of engagement. There's a rubric that they complete when they go into these classrooms . . . [T]hey use that data schoolwide to determine the level of engagement of the kids . . . [T]he level of engagement is higher at those schools where the kids are having success, or showing the most growth . . .

When Bill Lupini arrived in Brookline in 2004, some work had already been done to identify achievement gaps, but little action had been taken. His early communications in the district indicated that Lupini's push for action would face strong opposition from staff, parents, and community members who were happy with the status quo. Lupini pressed to show the extent of the achievement gaps and to understand underlying factors through inquiry:

> They had started something called the Equity Project. It was really more an examination of the problem. There'd been some effort to start to lay out some of the strategies, but that really started when I arrived . . . One of the things

that happened during my entry plan work was that a number of people tried to dissuade me from making this a major focus of the work . . . [I]t was easy to convince them that we needed to figure out what the other [in addition to state scores] measures [of gaps] were . . . We look at things like the placement of kids in upper level courses, their success in upper level courses, participation in extracurricular activities, [etc.].

Looking for and identifying gaps in various ways was often done quite publicly so that the community would understand where and how progress was being made. Doing so could be unpleasant when gains were not what were hoped for, but these superintendents were generally in agreement that publicizing data was an important part of the inquiry process that would ultimately lead to improvement.[5] Nerad explained:

Our graduation rate is going up, but the gaps aren't changing. They're going up for everybody, which is a good thing. But you know, we still have significant gaps with our kids of color . . . Embedded in that is a wide range of . . . outcome measures that would help us decide if we're making progress . . . and you'll see in that state of the district presentation . . . it's mixed . . . [Overall we're] not meeting targets . . . but we're using those specific measures that go beyond graduation rate, to define our progress.

Like Nerad, Jere Hochman identified many points of inquiry, searching for patterns of inequality and being open about where they exist:

We can look at the data, whether that's state tests, grades, participation in Advanced Placement classes. As you know, one of our ways to talk about this is that every setting in the school ought to look like what the school looks like. Whether it's the orchestra or the detention room or the cafeteria or the English class, it ought to be representative of the faces of our student body and I will tell you they're not. You can walk down the hall and tell what class you're looking into by what you see in the window. AP classes are predominantly white, etc. That . . . gets some attention, but I would say not a lot of action to turn that around specifically. There've been no targeted programs for that, except perhaps to try to ease the access.

If the differences between aspirations and outcomes are clear along different dimensions, then why, as Hochman notes, is action slow to follow? As discussed in chapter 1, organizational learning differentiates between single-loop and double-loop learning, and real change comes about only through the latter, in which organizations change key governing variables to work in new ways to solve problems. The superintendents knew that they needed to achieve double-loop learning, though they did not call it that. Nerad's discussion of graduation rates provides an example. Graduation rates overall improved, *but the gap remained.* This means that the Madison schools improved their ability to graduate all students, possibly with some single-loop learning solutions, but they may not have addressed the root causes for the *difference* in graduation rates between the majority and minority populations. We do not know the details of the strategy Nerad used, particularly timing of different measures. It is possible that key governing variables had in fact been changed, but that when we interviewed him insufficient time had elapsed to see the full fruits of implementation.

Changing governing variables is extremely difficult because in the disparity between what people espouse and what they do are uncomfortable issues that they would rather ignore—the undiscussables. As long as these remain buried, people will maintain the status quo to avoid dealing with them, and no real progress is possible. Lupini's example illuminates the point: although achievement gaps in Brookline were clearly recognized before he arrived, behavior had not substantially changed, and the gaps persisted. When Lupini began his tenure, he said, he was advised to avoid trying to do something about the situation—he sensed that he was expected to behave as if goals were being achieved and not to talk about the discrepancy. This is textbook behavior for organizations unable to engage in discussion of undiscussables—in this case, the persistence of gaps in achievement predicted by race—and thus achieve double-loop learning.[6]

Undiscussables

Anyone engaging in authentic inquiry will encounter undiscussables. The notion that people ignore or even actively resist organizational goals is not difficult to grasp. Such behavior is evident daily in schools, and it is not talked about because doing so would require a great deal of time and effort and likely generate conflict. In fact, this is exactly what Argyris found in his empirical work that tests the validity of organizational learning.[7] More difficult for us was differentiating undiscussables from mere disagreements or points of conflict in the superintendents' accounts of their efforts. It is safe to assume that the most difficult issues—e.g., institutional racism, inequitable opportunities, and scarce resources—had undiscussable elements in some districts while they were completely undiscussable in others. The superintendents themselves explained that the issues we examine next were difficult for them to address and yet had to be exposed and discussed before their districts could change governing variables and make meaningful progress on achievement gaps.

All thirteen superintendents demonstrated a remarkable willingness to address undiscussables in their quest to narrow achievement gaps in their school districts. Sherman took the most aggressive stance. His perspective was that racism, intentional and otherwise, perpetuated opportunity and achievement gaps based on race, income, and dominant language—a result he described as *disproportionality*:

> This city has [a] lot of racism . . . We're still very much a sleepy little Southern city that protects [the status quo and the myth of a city that overcame segregation] because of tourism, because we're so dependent on that . . . So I have taken that secrecy away from these questions and published as recently as two weeks ago a whole load about disproportionality, about achievement gaps, about who we are as a community, historically looking at 22 percent dropouts rates for Latino kids, and 19 percent of the kids dropping out of special ed. Why? Because they're black kids who are dropping out of special ed. The white kids are at 6 percent dropout rate. That has been tolerated. It's traditional. We see it in AP, we see it in SAT scores, we see it in courses kids take, we see it in grades, we see it in attendance, we see it in discipline. So for us, disproportionality has been a whole host of indicators. [Take] participation in sports. Got a baseball team—what do you see? It's a white team. Go to football—it's a black team.

Race as an undiscussable was by no means unique to Alexandria. Betty Feser wrestled with it more gently in Windsor with a mixed-race board. As described in chapter 2, African American members were concerned that comparing the scores of black and white students was tacitly racist because doing so implied that white students would inevitably perform better. On the other hand, white board members did not want to discuss race because they believed that attributing outcomes to race in any way was itself racist. One group felt aggrieved by how the students with whom they identified were perceived; another was unable or unwilling to see race as a factor. Adding to this mix, teachers held on to preconceptions about how different races of students would perform. That no one was willing to talk through such issues stalled progress on achievement gaps for a long time. Feser untangled the situation this way:

> The board of education has fundamental ideological differences around the issue of race, to the point where it has created real dysfunction on the board. There are some board members that believe it is racist to even look at scores by race. The premise is that it isn't an issue of race that creates the gap, it is family structure . . . I mean, it was just terrible what was happening. The issue of race is still there, you know. And they're not willing to talk about it . . . It has not been easy, and after nine years . . . I would say a large percentage of teachers . . . in their heart of hearts don't believe that the kids can do it, even though we're demonstrating, you know, increased performance.

Nerad and Osborne were both outspoken about the difficulty of talking about race in meaningful and productive ways, partly because their politically liberal communities tended to believe that they had sufficiently addressed race issues. Pederson acknowledged that despite years of work in the schools and community, perceptions and interests still sorted themselves out along racial lines, and he recognized some degree of fatigue with the topic and with achievement gaps more generally:

> [T]he African [American] community is certainly not satisfied with the amount or pace of progress. Periodically, that community kind of jells to send the message that we're not doing enough for their children and . . . questions whether we're sincere in our efforts, and do we have the knowledge and the commitment to . . . close the achievement gaps that are still readily there. I think there's a bit of pushback [from white parents] in that we've been focusing on this so long, that some . . . are ready for us to move on to something else. Why can't we pick up some other banner? . . . I think, in many cases, if you talk with parents of successful students, they're pretty quick to blame

the other children's parents about why those children are not successful; indicating they believe the schools can't do everything: "Parents have to carry their load and we shouldn't be blamed for those students' levels of achievement . . ." It just sort of erupts coincident with other things that are going on in society.

Linked to race and embedded in the tension between serving the needs of advanced students and helping those achieving at lower levels is the "zero-sum" undiscussable; that is, many parents believe there is only so much benefit available and any gain for another group's children is a loss for their own children. Parents of students in advanced programs such as AP or gifted and talented might express support for equity while suspecting that the school district is restricting opportunities for their children by allocating resources to closing achievement gaps. When access to advanced curricula is broadened, then parents worry that students who wouldn't previously have been admitted might compromise the quality of an advanced class. Mark Freeman spoke about this under-the-surface concern in Shaker Heights:

> Certainly a great deal of it . . . does deal back to what's the attitude the people bring into this situation and can you change it, and do you even know what it is? I think the answer is, you can . . . [Closing achievement gaps works] against the very difficult problem of "What does this do for my kids?" And "These children or those children are holding my child behind," and the view by some that any discipline problem or criminal problem is always "those people" . . . But, there's this constant battle of well, you know, the school district isn't what it used to be. And there's all these placeholders for . . . black people there.

This attitude is intensified in periods of economic downturn, as Hochman explains:

> I've got the data . . . that the community says this is important. But that's not to say there aren't a few who will make their side comments periodically, that "I don't understand why it takes a kid six years to learn English." "I don't understand why we're diverting all these resources into that school." You know, it gets down to economics. We're making cuts like everybody else, in spite of who we are. So, it's "You're going to cut my kid's enrichment class, you're going to cut back on music, but you're going to, you know, keep spending all these extra resources on ESL?"

Undiscussables were not unique to the community outside school walls. A major undiscussable was raised by Feser and explained in detail by Lupini and Sherman: Teachers were either unskilled, unmotivated, or both with respect to addressing the specific teaching and learning needs of minority students. Lupini struggled to raise this and other issues and faced some systemic challenges in his effort to change teacher practices:

[Why] the heck do you want to lift up the hood and look under the overall achievement profile? I mean, can't you just be satisfied with all these kids going to college, these terrific [state test] scores, terrific SAT scores? . . . [Teachers thought] we could program our way out of everything. [They believed] efforts that we're talking about here didn't have anything to do with my practice in the classroom. What we needed, you know, was an African American Scholars program, what we needed was a calculus project designed to get more kids in upper-level courses, what we needed was a literacy project, what we needed was steps to success to work with kids out of public housing. And of course, faculty would stand and applaud you when you said those kinds of things, but when you said it's going to require a real change in what you do in your classroom, the applause stopped . . . The difficult part that we struggled with year 3, year 4, as we started to make the change from programming to let's talk about the classroom, was how to continue to make people who'd been told forever that they were great not feel like we were telling them . . . that they were terrible, while we were challenging them to do this work better. And that continues to be a large part of the challenge for us.

Osborne faced a similar situation in South Orange and Maplewood. He was fortunate to have teachers willing to help him open up the undiscussable of teacher attitudes toward certain students:

There's a couple of small groups of teachers with whom I'm in some informal, you know, collusion around these issues. And, they say, "Listen, the culture of our secondary schools is really a color-blind liberal teaching culture. They will claim they treat every kid the same and they don't see color. And every time somebody comes and says race has something to do with what we're doing and how we perceive each other and kids, they just wait it out . . ." We've been planning and trying to make sure that we structure the conversation such that no one can wait it out.

Numerous undiscussables pervade these superintendents' districts, and they are embedded particularly densely in the areas of race, resources, and teacher practice. All of the superintendents addressed undiscussables they believed were important enough to warrant the cost of backlash, though some, like Osborne, were subtle about how they did so. They all understood that these issues needed to be aired if practices were to change. In the language of organizational learning, changing governing variables requires breaking down the wall of undiscussables. The centrality of undiscussables to making organizational change is amply demonstrated by the superintendents' experiences related above, and by the fact that twelve of the thirteen superintendents specifically referred to surfacing undiscussables as a focus of their work.

Governing Variables

Governing variables anchor the status quo. Many of these explicit and implicit rules, and corresponding characteristics of the status quo such as community commitment to integration and equity, were valued by the superintendents. But other governing variables were impediments to closing achievement gaps. The most effective and long-lasting changes will occur when governing variables are changed and double-loop learning is achieved.[8] Contrary to organizational learning practice, but consistent with common wisdom about leadership and change, some of the superintendents recognized changes that needed to be made and took action soon after they entered the school district. This pattern often manifests in mandated change, and subsequent mopping-up operations to deal with fallout from undiscussables. Hardy Murphy provides a clear example that describes need, opportunity, and consequences:

> The struggle there I had was really making transitions into a very assertive changing of the way things were done, which was a challenging of the status quo. So part of it had to do with the district had been without the superintendent for a couple of years . . . Part of the challenge I had was creating a school district rather than a district of schools through the creation of systems through which you would advance the cause of equity . . . Changing the district in that way created somewhat of a challenge, because what people

then saw was that there was a kind of a direction, especially from the central office, that they hadn't received before. The district, I think, and everyone had kind of recoiled from that, because there hadn't been much—in some ways a laissez-faire approach to things. And I don't mean that in the sense that there was a lack of effort. I think everyone was trying really hard. But . . . coming up with a coherent effort was the struggle . . . One of the first things that I did in this process, and I think that did create some resistance, was, in the first year we stopped pulling students out of reading for reading support . . . The other thing that happened is that I changed the structure, the process for setting [evaluation] goals . . . I established uniform goals for everyone across the district, including the principals, to focus on student achievement . . .

Much of the progress reported in the introduction occurred as a result of changing governing variables. One of the most common changes made by the superintendents was to unify school curricula, the "moving from a district of schools to a school district." Another was steadfastly presenting and analyzing data that show differences between identifiable groups, even when there was resistance, such as in Windsor or Brookline. Further, digging under the data to examine evidence of institutional racism was a major change in districts such as Chapel Hill-Carrboro, South Orange and Maplewood, and Alexandria.

Judy Wilson and Betty Feser were equally assertive about changing key governing variables, but they also took a slower approach by starting with data collection, analysis, and communication. They were more inclined to build consensus regarding problem definition before changing governing variables. Common to both Wilson and Feser was changing the rules regarding allocation of resources. They were adamant that their districts would strategically support students who traditionally struggled through their systems. For Wilson, this was ensuring pre-kindergarten for children in poverty, even in the face of declining resources. For Feser, it was, among other things, assuring proportional representation in academic recognitions and in college attendance.

Double-Loop Learning

Did changes in governing variables persist, and did these lead to meaningful changes in practices, behaviors, and attitudes in schools? Most of the superintendents would answer in the affirmative, and such changes are elaborated in chapters 5 and 6. Two examples at this point provide a preview of more detailed accounts of changes resulting from double-loop learning. The first is Mark Freeman's effort to open access to challenging curricula:

> I said that no longer could there be prerequisites for any Advanced Placement or honors class at the high school. That it was all open enrollment. Of course, you know, there was, "Oh my God, this [is] terrible. Standards [are] falling apart, the place will crumble." Well, of course it made very little, if any, difference in the composition of the classes and who took them, because the students know the difficulty . . . We still don't have it. It's still disproportionate . . . It's changed. It's improved because the teachers take pride in it. Now they know and they buy into it. They want it too. It's certainly much better. But boy, it's slow and incremental.

Neil Pederson describes double-loop learning with respect to race after many years' effort:

> So now we were more focused on equity, opportunity, institutionalized racism, dealing with relationships, perceptions, [and] we've continued that work . . . It's more than ten years later, and probably in more recent years we've shifted more to culturally proficient practices . . . As difficult as [equitable programming and] the work on race and equity is, that certainly would be among the three [accomplishments] that I would [emphasize]. I am proud we took this on. I think it spoke highly of our district, of our community, of our leadership. And I think it really has made a difference. When people come to our district, they say no one else has these kinds of conversations.

CONCLUSION

Organizational capacity, stability, and learning are tightly interrelated and interdependent. Capacity and stability provide a context that enables learning. At the same time, learning enhances capacity and may, because it opens up undiscussables, serve as a destabilizing influence. As a systems approach to change and improvement within school districts, organizational learning is challenging yet filled with high potential. It operates like a dynamo in our conceptual framework: the learning process generates data, analysis, and, ultimately, interventions instrumental in closing achievement gaps. But the dynamo is not completely within the control of leadership. The possibility for learning antithetical to superintendents' visions and goals is real. Results are often slow to materialize, requiring patience within schools and the community and longevity of service for the superintendent. Perhaps the most important factor is the need for superintendents to see their districts as systems that require continual nurturing of capacity, stability, and learning. Chapter 4 elaborates how the superintendents cultivated learning organizations by exploring how they collaborated with their school boards and communities their systems served.

CHAPTER FOUR

Aligning the Perspectives of the School Board, Superintendent, and Community

As the appointed executive of a democratically elected school board, the superintendent is naturally embedded in electoral and organizational politics. This has been the lot of the US superintendent[1] ever since the position was invented early in the nineteenth century.[1] Periodically, large-city mayors have taken over school boards and played an important role in appointing board members and, by extension, superintendents, thus altering the politics of the position. Such was not the case for our thirteen superintendents, however. All were appointed by elected boards whose members served four-year terms, often staggered. The superintendents were acutely aware that they served at the pleasure of the boards, which could alter their agendas—and their careers—on very short notice. The political realities of their service as educators was one reason they made efforts to work closely with their boards and the broader communities in which their schools were embedded to align vision, goals, and energy toward closing achievement gaps.

This work was neither easy nor straightforward. As representatives of various interests within their communities, school board members bridged from the school district to the community, and if they represented divergent interests, they might be at loggerheads. Similarly, those competing interests could play out in the community and take the form of conflicting expectations for the superintendent and individual board members. Common sense and classic organization theory would suggest that organizations with greater integration of beliefs and operations across their units and in relation to their external environments will be more successful than organizations that lack such integration.[2]

Sometimes superintendents were helped by their boards to promote their equity message; in other cases, superintendents reached around their boards to spotlight community voices not well represented on the boards. Whatever the case, school boards constitute a critical influence in the district context, as indicated in figure 2.1. They are both from the community and distinct from it because of their special relationship to the superintendent. For the thirteen superintendents and their boards alike, the community they served embodied opportunities and threats that could help or hinder social justice work. The one certainty was the superintendents needed to work in harmony with their boards.

SYNCING WITH THE BOARD

In the twelve years of his superintendency in Arlington, Smith worked with the board to formulate and articulate academic and affective strategies to narrow achievement gaps. Even as board members turned over during his tenure, Smith and the board were aligned on their gap-closing mission.[3] Pat Murphy, who followed Smith as superintendent in 2009, explained the degree that the achievement gap had worked its way into the thought patterns of the board with a vignette from early on in his term:

> I recall very specifically when I came here initially and I was making some introductory comments. I made the comment that my personal goal was to continue to close the achievement gap, as it had been a tradition here in Arlington. I was sitting in a group with some board members and one of the board members very politely tugged on my jacket. I leaned over and she said [whispering], "I just want to tell you that we're not interested in closing the achievement gap here in Arlington. We're interested in eliminating it." She said, "You may want to change just how you're presenting on that."

Naturally, not all the school boards showed such fervent commitment to narrowing or eliminating achievement gaps. Although support varied from district to district, superintendents acknowledged the importance of having their boards pull together with them on the issue. To make this possible, they were careful to apply for positions in districts where the school board shared their social justice agendas, which may be easier to discern in MSAN member districts. Six were emphatic that they would not have taken or stayed in their positions without strong complementary intentions from the school boards in their districts. Brian Osborne describes the importance to him of this shared vision:

> The board in their very ad for superintendent said . . . their first priority was to [find] someone who was committed to narrowing the achievement gap. For the board to put out an ad like that in a diverse suburb like South Orange and Maplewood, I was at least intrigued enough to go and see if they were serious. A couple of conversations later, I was superintendent of schools there.

Hardy Murphy, who had worked for years on school desegregation issues, elaborated on the importance of the board's commitment to making progress toward social justice and explained how he perceived their role as his partners in the effort:

> When I came to Evanston, [closing the achievement gap] was mentioned as one of the issues that that board and the community were concerned with. It was kind of just a natural transition . . . I came into the district with that charge from the school board to address the achievement gap in some way.

Dan Nerad shared a similar perspective:

> I believe there is a significant role relative to board policy, especially around equity issues, that needs to be the focus of the board in addressing achievement gap issues . . . That is, what do we do with policies to create as much access for kids to more enriched learning opportunities? And do we have policies that prevent that from happening?

Nurturing and expanding the school board's understanding of what would be needed to close achievement gaps was an ongoing preoccupation for Hardy Murphy (as noted in chapter 3) and several of the other superintendents. Educating the board was driven by the need to turn aspirations into concrete policies and actions and the natural turnover of board members that necessitated revisiting vision, values, and goals so that new members could understand and support the direction the district was taking. One important means for board members to educate themselves regarding equity issues was the MSAN school board assembly discussed in chapter 1. MSAN was therefore one means of helping boards and prospective superintendents engage in a common discourse. Sue Zurvalec described her efforts to move the Farmington school board from interesting conversations to action, beginning from the time before she was promoted to superintendent:

> We brought [Rossi Ray-Taylor, the Ann Arbor Public Schools superintendent] in to talk with our school board about joining MSAN and we believed it was the next right step for us. What we really needed now was to focus on student achievement and the gaps. We focused on diversity as an [inclusive] culture and embracing it as a strength, but it was still more about being nice to each other than it was really about getting to the root cause of this and how do we fix it . . . Race is the significant component because of the way race is perceived in our culture. Particularly, I have to say, in metropolitan Detroit . . . We have talked about the fact that Detroit itself . . . is the most segregated [metropolitan] area in the nation. It's also the most diverse. So we have segregation and we have diversity. And in our community, we are aiming for true integration and not to become what some other places have become in that area.

Betty Feser's board was not always in agreement on achievement gap-related issues. She and the other superintendents understood that when board members held conflicting views, the differences needed to be worked through so that the board and superintendent could speak with one voice on this very challenging topic. Feser was clear that she needed to resolve differences on the board before Windsor was able to make meaningful progress. We strongly suspect that when boards were unable or unwilling to agree on the nature of or appropriate responses to achievement gaps that there was increased likelihood for the superintendent to leave or to be told to leave.

Certainly, the character of the various boards influenced the progress of narrowing achievement gaps. Pat Murphy described his board's passionate commitment to eliminating achievement gaps in Arlington. Dan Nerad found strong contrasts between Green Bay and Madison. Even though both were MSAN districts, and both boards were proponents of the MSAN agenda, Nerad found it easier to engage the Green Bay than the Madison board in discussions about quality instruction for all students and about achievement gaps. He attributed that difference, in part, to a more bimodal distribution of family income in Madison than in Green Bay. Jere Hochman described the Amherst-Pelham board as having racial equity "in its DNA," a contrast with the St. Louis suburbs he first served as superintendent and Bedford, where he was when we interviewed him. Board politics shifted underneath Mort Sherman when he was in Cherry Hill, causing his departure. But when he brought a very similar agenda to Alexandria (not an MSAN district until he became superintendent), the board embraced it.

Board qualities naturally derive from the communities in which they are situated and the local politics that create them. Many of the communities these superintendents served had long histories of efforts to integrate, equalize educational opportunities, and pursue social justice. Arlington, Shaker Heights, Princeton, and Brookline are prominent examples. All had legacies of separation and protection of wealthy enclaves followed by efforts to rise above segregation and white flight. For example, Arlington prided itself on being the first school district in Virginia to integrate its schools, yet consequent to its integration plan, its elected school board was eliminated by the state legislature for flying in the face of the state's "massive resistance" to implementing the *Brown* decision.

As noted above, superintendents who based their professional and personal identities on the pursuit of social justice were naturally attracted to work for the boards that emerged out of these contexts. For example, the first major issue which Smith faced as he entered Arlington in 1997 was the overturning by a federal district court of an affirmative action measure that placed students of color at two choice schools in the district—the kind of fight that he and the board that hired him were willing to pursue. Thus, matches between superintendents and their boards tended to be strong, perhaps resulting in the unusual longevity of this group of thirteen superintendents. Common understanding and forward motion were not automatic, however, and the superintendents had to work to establish and maintain both.

COMMUNITY—ANOTHER PILLAR OF SUPPORT

The values and aspirations of elected school boards will likely echo, at least in part, the voting public they serve. Thus, the social justice experiences and reactions of the communities in which school districts are embedded are important contextual influences. Mark Freeman's long service in Shaker Heights was well aligned with community values that were rooted in decades of commitment to maintaining an ethnically and racially integrated community. Both before and during his tenure, the district faced the unusual challenge of including a part of the city of Cleveland. This made equity issues both more urgent and more difficult because of housing patterns that may have isolated impoverished students in the community and in schools. Economically disadvantaged students were more likely to be African American, adding the overlay of race to the challenge of providing equitable educational opportunities:

> [I]n the mid-50s, early '60s, Shaker Heights began to integrate. Now, prior to that there were Catholics and Jews, and those populations grew substantially. But this was the first movement of African American families outside of the central city to the suburbs . . . I think that for the most part, this was a community that rose to this challenge. It's an interesting legacy . . . My kind of history with school boards is that they have been very helpful with this. They have seen it as a brand for the school district to be able to do this. An area of pride.

Judy Wilson describes a similar combined effect among the Princeton community, the school board, and her leadership:

> The support for equity has at least for the last fifteen years been broad-based, community based as well as board based. My predecessor had certainly begun work in that area, but was only in the district for three and a half years. [He]

had been a member of MSAN and had made some strong commitments . . . So, it wasn't something I had to bring to the table new.

Moving from general community support of the school district's effort to narrow achievement gaps into specific actions reveals a more difficult and complex problem for superintendents. The power differentials discussed in chapter 3 led to some finger-pointing about what parents of struggling students were or were not doing. Such talk was not productive for the larger agenda, so when that kind of conflict emerged, superintendents tended to manage it and the messier parts of community involvement by refocusing efforts on what the schools *could* do and making clear that policing parenting practices was not on the agenda. Where superintendents appeared to have the greatest success in mobilizing the community to act was working with larger entities that represented core community interests. When Bill Lupini arrived in Brookline, the community was well positioned for action on achievement gap issues. It had a prior history as an MSAN district and long-term working relationships with community-based foundations. Lupini spoke extensively about coordinating community interests and community resources to support the legacy gap-closing agenda to which previous superintendents, along with the Brookline school board, had devoted their efforts:

METCO is the program that allows students from Boston to come to suburban school systems. They're bused. It's been going on since the late '60s, and we're the second-largest program [in the Boston area]. We had a lot of METCO families involved, we had a lot of support from one of those foundations . . . who actually were funding some of the initiatives . . . [T]he [Brookline] Education Foundation, which has always been on the page with us about, "How do we fund your initiatives?" "How do we participate with you?" "What's the professional development you need us to support?" and then give us the hook to go out fund raise for it. Within the last [six months] or so, the Twenty-First Century Fund . . . came and said, "So how do we work together better? Because this isn't working. What we're doing now, us kind of funding things and then coming to the district and saying why aren't you picking up some of our initiatives after three years, four years, five years?" Because they don't fit our mission, that's why. They said, "How do we do that better?"

Lupini described his efforts to bring community resources and influence into the school district in a manner more traditional, more directly education-focused, than Dan Nerad in Madison and Mort Sherman in Alexandria. As previously noted, Nerad identified access to health care as an important opportunity gap that was impacting student achievement (we elaborate on this in Chapter 6). Having cultivated strong support from the school board, Sherman reached out to community groups that he believed would resonate with his anti-racist message focused on improving educational opportunities for traditionally underserved students. He recounted building a political base among typically dissatisfied sectors of the community that would provide support for his effort to eliminate disproportionality—an initiative that may have seemed controversial to those from inside the district and in the community who believed the schools were working well and that he was being unnecessarily confrontational:

> I have now formed partnerships with NAACP and what we call here Tenants and Workers United, which is a political and labor activist group over in [an area of Alexandria that borders a neighboring community that has] historically work[ed] with our cabbies, but have now become the voice of Latino communication. We have signed an MOU [memorandum of understanding] among these organizations to work with me. So we're not feuding. We're holding monthly meetings, community meetings, to talk about disproportionality, the discipline issues. These groups are saying, "We're on board with what the superintendent's doing. We want to see this change." Boy, has that coalesced folks in the community, as you can imagine. So that leverage is very strong.

By harmonizing the focus and interests of the school board and influential community groups, Sherman was able to stabilize his political base and that of his incumbent board members. Whether these alliances resulted in tangible resources and/or action for his equity agenda we do not know.

ON THE TIGHTROPE

Although some communities served by the superintendents were deliberately and self-consciously integrated, most had evolved to be more diverse. This trend was due more to economic circumstances than values held by community members. In all cases, there was substantial board and community support for making educational opportunities more equitable across the entire student population. Equally prevalent, however, was a tension or ambivalence about the equity agenda, usually expressed as wealthier parents fearing that their children would lose resources, opportunity, or quality of educational experiences as a result of scarce resources being poured into gap-closing strategies.

Expanding on the argument about how superintendents balanced the various interests against each other in an effort to maintain district stability, we use the metaphor of tightrope walking. The superintendents needed to be vigilant about their messaging and meaningful involvement of multiple constituencies. They understood that the school board and the community they represented needed to value the same educational ends, or board politics would cause the end of their superintendency one way or another—either through the election of new board members with different agendas or conflict with the incumbent board. Either way, the superintendents' contracts were on the line.

Superintendents typically praised their communities and their boards who desired to address inequities in their educational systems, the more so as it was these perspectives that in nearly every case drew the superintendents to the districts they served. Nevertheless, the hard work of designing and implementing gap-closing tactics and programs caused tension, whether because of strained resources, disappointing outcomes, or other factors. Thus, superintendents often spoke of setbacks in their efforts to cultivate community support or bring critical resources into the school district.

Most of the superintendents were reluctant to criticize the board members with whom they were currently working or the citizens who provided board members'—and by extension, superintendents'—political bases. We were able to infer that there was more tension in some districts and less in others. We have featured Feser's struggle to get agreement with her board because she was the most outspoken on this issue, possibly because at the time of her interview, she had already announced her departure to Milford Public Schools. Feser's persistence and patience—and some degree of frustration—in working with a board whose members did not entirely agree with one another or with her vision may be seen as representative of the kind of struggle all superintendents deal with over time. Feser's ability ultimately to find a way to move the board off of their disagreement over how achievement gaps should be defined toward making change within the district is a testament to her political skill and the value of longevity in the role. Feser serves as an optimistic example to other superintendents in this regard.

It is easy to attribute too much control to superintendents as the chief executives of their school systems. As many of their stories illustrate, several factors are beyond their direct control. Even when apparently successful in implementing innovative programs, the superintendents were sometimes stymied in their equity efforts by privileged families' additional efforts to get a leg up. From one perspective, this might be seen as a positive outcome because wealthier families stayed committed to the public schools. On the other hand, gaps remained as Nerad observed with respect to graduation rates in Madison (see chapter 3). Pederson explains this phenomenon from the perspective of Chapel Hill-Carrboro:

> [W]hile we've added resources and opportunities for students within our schools, I would say that parents of means have been able to provide even more resources for their students, for their children, to be successful academically, athletically, culturally. It's a bit like an arms race, and I'd have to say that wealthy families have more arms than we do. So when we're trying to level the playing field, I think society keeps making it less and less level . . . I think it's unrealistic to think that doesn't make any difference. And to a great extent that inequity still has significant racial overtones to it.

It is possible to sense both weariness and optimism from Pederson, on the cusp of his retirement after a nineteen-year tenure as superintendent. Some of the other superintendents also expressed the view that different segments of their communities simply didn't understand each other very well, no matter how well intentioned they may have been. Osborne commented on the way some members of the community, despite voicing as-

pirations for social justice appeared unaware of the conditions experienced
by less advantaged members of their community:

> In the community where I'm working now, where the majority of our kids,
> not the super majority but the majority of kids, are coming to school from
> households of college-educated families who read to them every night and
> tell them that they're going to go to college one day and that they damn
> well better do their homework. The adult community within our schools
> [believes] that that's the norm. And the kids who are coming from other
> experiences without that kind of home support, somehow something's
> wrong with them. It's a very difficult conversation to have in our school
> community.

Not far away, in Princeton, Wilson felt the tension of sectors of the
community not understanding what was really happening in the schools
and being skeptical about progress with previously underserved students.
But on balance, she viewed the community as less judgmental than South
Orange and Maplewood and more consistently supportive of the equity
agenda:

> There's a minority education committee that's a community-based group
> that's existed for at least a decade . . . It's had mediocre points and low points,
> mostly because it's not a board committee . . . It changes from year to year.
> It's not clear in its actions so it can, at its worst point, deteriorate to "We'll
> meet once a month on Monday nights and we'll just tell war stories . . ." At
> its strongest point, a couple white papers, a couple position papers, a couple
> of recommendations to the board that have been strong over the years and
> good. For the rest of the community, Princeton's a very, very generous place.
> For much of the community, it's about providing supports and services, most
> of it anonymously, to anybody who has a need in the town . . . The board has
> a policy that no matter what trip—to Philadelphia or Barcelona, spring train-
> ing or a local museum—everybody goes whether they can pay or not. Choir
> just came back from Barcelona, you know—five kids couldn't pay. Everybody
> made sure that they were covered. Mostly parent donations . . . And it's not
> just about writing checks. I think there is a deep community belief system,
> and I think Princeton's been built upon it for a long time, that there's open ac-
> cess, there's open support to walk through this point of access and everybody
> deserves it.

The superintendents' reflections on working with their communities all showed the tightrope each walked over a pit of power struggles, jealousy, fear, and white privilege. There was also a clear sense that this was part of the job. As superintendents, they were leaders in their communities and had a responsibility to address the needs of multiple constituencies, bring additional resources to bear on education by any means possible, and keep the equity discussion prominent.

CONCLUSION

Superintendents work at a nexus between community politics and public service in an effort to pursue educational goals. The superintendents represented in this book took on the highly charged issue of making education more equitable by ensuring excellence and maximum opportunities for all students. Noble as this intent appears on its face, making progress was difficult because of entrenched beliefs, scarce resources, and sincere differences of opinion. The superintendents aspired to use their boards and their communities as assets and allies to forward the cause of social justice.

Our superintendents are not a representative sample, because we chose them based on their districts' membership in MSAN and their having served at least two years in their position. This strategy imposes a limitation on our study—we do not know the experiences of superintendents and districts for which the pursuit of equity led to different outcomes, nor do we know the perspectives of MSAN superintendents who had been removed or removed themselves from their positions. Likewise, we do not know why some districts such as Berkeley, Columbia, White Plains, and Cherry Hill chose to leave the network. What we do know is that not all communities, districts, and superintendents are able and/or willing to address achievement gaps as our participating superintendents have.

When superintendents were able to forge agreement between the school board, the community, and themselves about a way forward, they often turned to strengthening the teacher corps as one of the necessary steps to achieving equity. Chapter 5 describes this process.

CHAPTER FIVE

Building Teacher Capacity

Although they varied in their approaches to professional development, all of the superintendents we interviewed perceived building teacher capacity as an essential step on their paths to achieving greater equality of educational opportunity for students. Improving teachers' skills, knowledge, and classroom practices was critical to both narrowing achievement gaps and ensuring that promising approaches to teaching and learning would be sustained over time. In terms of our conceptual framework, professional development comprised a set of critical interventions resulting from organizational learning and intended to benefit minority students.

Professional development that expands teachers' repertoires to address a range of student needs is crucial to the creation of equitable learning. Many, if not most, teachers lack adequate skills and knowledge to meet the needs of ever more diverse student populations, so finding ways to provide PD was very much on superintendents' minds. Knapp's definition of professional development places it in the broader universe of adult learning that demonstrates a range of possibilities for teacher growth:

> Opportunities for professional learning are many and varied, far more so than is generally embraced by common usage of the term *professional development*. A more inclusive and productive conception of opportunities for professional learning assumes that this learning takes place both within practice itself (as practicing professionals experiment with and draw conclusions about their daily work) and in settings outside of practice, in formalized structures

designed for professional learning (e.g., workshops, courses) as well as various informal settings (reading journals, spontaneous conversations with colleagues) . . . and in activities primarily designed for professional learning (usually designated as "professional development") . . .[1]

The superintendents used a similarly broad array of PD opportunities to pursue equity, but a number of them first created common curricula and installed instruction and assessment aligned with curricula as critical prerequisites that would help to focus teacher learning in the most important areas. Professional development concentrated on enhancing instruction, creating professional learning communities to improve instruction and assessment, opening up access to rigorous academic experiences for all students, and augmenting cultural competence. These prominent interventions were intended to change the direction of teaching and learning.

Training in general procedures designed to increase the effectiveness and differentiation of instruction was seen as important in most of the districts. Several superintendents also pushed for professional development related to expectations that affect the treatment of students of color and their likelihood of participating in rigorous academic experiences. Some sustained major efforts over a number of years to confront thorny issues of race and equity as part of the process of addressing expectations and access to high-quality curricula.

SUPPORTING COMMON CURRICULA, INSTRUCTION, AND ASSESSMENT

At least six of the superintendents (Feser, Hardy Murphy, Wilson, Lee, Lupini, and Osborne) came to districts that lacked common curricula across schools, and correcting this was among their earliest actions, given the difficulty of introducing changes to decrease opportunity gaps when each school was designing its own curriculum. They perceived that schools determining their own curricula would result in an uneven quality of learning experiences across schools, and that the schools with larger proportions of students experiencing lower achievement would offer fewer opportunities for academically rigorous experiences. The same problems would manifest within single diverse schools as well, when less challenging curricula would be offered to students expected to perform less well. Thus, the intent was to ensure that all students have access to a common set of worthwhile, rigorous experiences and that variation in the outcomes would depend less on race, language, or wealth than on interest and amount of effort.

Betty Feser referred to the Windsor district in her first years there as a "system of schools" as opposed to a "school system." Her first moves included a major push to establish a common curriculum in literacy and ramped-up professional development to implement it. She also used instructional coaches to provide small group and individual assistance to teachers. Professional development focused on the literacy curriculum was later complemented by a new emphasis on preparing and helping teachers analyze student achievement data tied to the new curriculum. Concentrating initially on elementary schools, she moved toward the high school level later in her tenure.

Hardy Murphy used language similar to Feser's when describing the situation he initially faced in the preK–8 Evanston-Skokie schools: "It was a district of schools, and within the schools, the classrooms were pretty much going on their own way . . . they had [adopted] site-based management . . . to the extreme." Murphy focused first on the development of districtwide improvement and equity goals applied to each school and classroom. How to realize these goals then became the content for newly established professional development days involving districtwide grade-level and content area sessions treating common curricular and instructional expectations. After forging revised curricula, Murphy turned his attention to creating common assessments and how to use them.

Describing the situation in Princeton when she began her tenure as superintendent, Judy Wilson explained the difficulties caused by the absence of a coherent common curriculum, particularly for children who performed less well:

> One of the things that our really able, eager learners didn't suffer as much from, but I knew everyone else did, was the fact that there was no identified K–5 or K–12 curriculum seven years ago. Every teacher chose—not just every

building or every grade level, [but] every *teacher* K–5 chose—whatever he or she wanted to do for reading and mathematics. A really well-grounded, bright, able learner was able to navigate that pretty well with different texts and different teacher vocabulary, different patterns of instruction, but even that was challenging for most people. And for kids who were struggling, I have to imagine that that was pretty much a nightmare.

Wilson initiated and shepherded the installation of a coherent curriculum and secured the professional development for its implementation in both language arts and mathematics.

In Paradise Valley, Jim Lee, like Hardy Murphy, focused on alignment of goals, instruction, and assessment:

> The formula is this: . . . if we have kids in schools where the curriculum is real clear and consistent and well laid out through the use of curriculum maps, and there are formative assessments attached to that curriculum and those assessments are monitored on a regular daily, weekly basis, and there are interventions, and—this is a key—[a model for helping] those kids when they start to fall behind or they don't understand a concept or they're not grasping a standard, that is where you can close an achievement gap. It's as simple as that. And I'll debate that with anybody, because we're seeing that in our district.

Within this framework, Lee also talked about using externally developed programs in mathematics and the Instructional Practices Inventory to support the common curriculum. Implementing these programs required considerable professional development, elaborated in the next section.

When Brian Osborne arrived in South Orange and Maplewood, he was astonished to find that the district did not have an English language arts curriculum:

> I was just totally flabbergasted. Who decides what the kids . . . read? The teacher does. So you had the same variability that every system has, but compounded by the fact 'that there were no consistent expectations for even what a third grader would read.

In the interest of creating a more uniform approach across the district, Osborne and key staff members adopted a reader-writer workshop approach, including the use of "mentor texts" to provide exemplars of various kinds of writing and organized professional development to support the implementation effort. In 2011, he was working on implementing a common approach and materials for teaching mathematics, and in particular exploring adoption of a set of math texts and materials known as Everyday Mathematics, developed at the University of Chicago.[2] Similar to Lee and others, Osborne counted on extensive professional development to ensure successful and consistent implementation of common curricula.

Mort Sherman, like Osborne, recounted his consternation at finding that Alexandria lacked a common curriculum:

> It's shocking to me, having been a curriculum coordinator starting in 1979. There was no curriculum here. There were pacing guides for [state-mandated Standards of Learning tests]. [But] no curriculum . . . therefore, ELL and special education and general education curriculum were all in separate silos . . . I removed the silos and put in one high-level curriculum . . . That is the most meaningful thing I've done, and I think the community would recognize it.

Implementing Sherman's new high-level curriculum necessitated professional development. That initiative was added to the other PD programs provided by the district.

Brookline Public Schools started applying a more systematic approach to program design, professional development, and assessment after Bill Lupini took the helm. In contrast to previous improvement efforts, which had been driven by individual teachers, principals, and schools, Lupini's approach called for adherence to the districtwide strategic plan, emphasizing the need to align teachers' skills and knowledge with the curriculum:

> We were a district that was really good at one time at providing professional development that reflected peoples' interest. So the person who wanted to go do XYZ in Europe . . . the foundation or the district supported that. That's gone. Now it's, "This is the strategic plan, this is what a Brookline teacher is, this is what we support, this is what we provide, this is what we require, but we will support the heck out of you around that . . ." but that's what it takes to teach here.

PROFESSIONAL DEVELOPMENT FOR PROGRAM IMPLEMENTATION

Most of the school districts organized professional development in the service of implementing new or revised programs, including creating equitable curricula, removing barriers to advanced classes, and improving student achievement in specific content areas. Some PD was homegrown, and some was developed by external sources. To ensure quality implementation over time, more than just the initial burst of professional development was required, and given the turnover of faculty and staff, there were always new people who would need the original and follow-up learning opportunities. As Pederson suggested about his experience in Chapel Hill-Carrboro, planning for continuity of implementation of a range of programs had to be intentional, from revisions in the teaching of gifted and talented to work with special education students, as well as maintaining a focus on culturally proficient instruction:

> In order for some of these practices or philosophies to permeate the system, it takes a number of years. In some cases, we're still at it ten years later. It probably shouldn't take that long, but the reality is, some of that training just never goes away when you have 10–15 percent turnover and you're a growing school system. [Even though the enrollment] growth rate has slowed down now . . . every year, we've had 150 new teachers out of a thousand, so you can't say, "Well, we did that five years ago, we've moved on to something else." So, there's some continuity that's necessary.

Lee's approach to professional development in Paradise Valley focused on the programs he introduced to meet specific student needs. He appeared most enthusiastic about applying the principles promoted by an initiative called Beat the Odds, jointly sponsored by Arizona State University and the Center for the Future of Arizona, which had been adopted in three of the district's schools.[3] This program used the comparative procedures applied by Jim Collins in his book *Good to Great*, which studied why some American businesses rose far above their peers.[4] By comparing high-performing companies with less successful companies with similar characteristics, Collins was able to uncover a set of principles that differentiated the high-performing from the low-performing companies, and to organize these principles into three categories: disciplined thought, people and action. Beat the Odds conducted research in twelve Arizona elementary and middle schools with large Latino student populations that were performing well in mathematics and language arts and compared them with twelve demographically similar schools that were performing poorly, then studied the schools to discover the differences that appeared to explain the discrepancy.[5] Lee implemented the findings in the three Paradise schools that participated in the initiative and in extensive teacher training. He reported that they were performing at unexpectedly high levels. The three schools adopted the six practices that the researchers concluded explained the higher performance of the Beat the Odds schools.[6]

Over the years, many of the MSAN districts adopted at least three national initiatives: Advancement Via Individual Determination (AVID), Read 180, and the Tripod Project. AVID provides training to help teachers prepare students underrepresented at four-year colleges and universities to be college-ready and close achievement gaps. Most of the adopting districts paid for the training and provided AVID classes that served students who demonstrated great potential but faced a variety of barriers to getting ready for college.[7] Read 180 is a computer-assisted individualized reading program designed to help struggling readers.[8] Ron Ferguson's Tripod Project focused on using student feedback to teachers regarding their teaching practices, their content knowledge and their relationships with students (see chapter 1 for more detail).[9]

MSAN actively conducted information dissemination and research initiatives for the Read 180 and the Tripod programs. Districts adopted AVID on their own, but the program was a common topic of presentations and discussion at MSAN gatherings.

These are only three examples among many of the interventions adopted by the superintendents. Other prominent examples mentioned by multiple superintendents and probably used by others included Sheltered Instruction Observation Protocol (SIOP), an approach to instruction involving professional development, designed to help English language learners perform well in school across subjects, that was used by Arlington,

Bedford and Princeton. Arlington and Princeton both adopted the Teachers College Workshop Model, a professional development approach that encourages academic rigor and advances the success of struggling learners in literacy, Revamped approaches to teacher evaluation based on Charlotte Danielson's framework were implemented in Windsor, South Orange and Maplewood, and Arlington.[10]

Consistent with their organizational approaches to improving equity in their districts, the superintendents actively supported implementation of new programs with targeted professional development. Superintendents agreed that when adopting an intervention aimed at specific root causes of inequities in their systems, teacher capacity needed to be addressed to help those interventions to be as effective as possible. Less important than the specific programs was the idea that superintendents banked on these interventions as logical responses to what data analysis revealed would yield narrowed achievement gaps. They linked their various solutions to the reasons for inequity as they understood them (e.g., chaotic curricula, learning gaps, or unequal college readiness) and supported their proposed solutions through their control of district resources, attention, and rhetoric focused on teacher professional development.

PROFESSIONAL LEARNING COMMUNITIES AND DISTRIBUTED LEADERSHIP

Professional development was also fostered by the creation and operation of professional learning communities (PLCs) in several districts. In an apparent contradiction, some of the superintendents who were concerned about implementing more uniform curricula and instruction also favored assigning responsibility for the assessment and analysis of both student achievement and instructional procedures to teacher teams organized by grade levels and/or subjects taught. Betty Feser, Brian Osborne, and Sue Zurvalec expressed strong convictions regarding the power of PLCs to improve instruction (as did Jim Lee indirectly through support of the Beat the Odds practices) and also saw them as a means to cultivate greater consistency in instruction. All three believed an effective strategy for school district professional development resides in practices that, in Knapp's words, ". . . strengthen professional communities and engage them in professional learning activities."[11] Having established the clear mission of eliminating achievement gaps, superintendents thought that gap-closing strategies were more likely to succeed if leadership were distributed to PLCs. There, teachers were encouraged to work together to develop common practices for analysis of student work, delivery of instruction, and assessment of results. During the years in which these superintendents implemented PLCs, the research on whether the activities of such learning communities resulted in greater student achievement was still in its infancy. Later findings appear to support the faith of these superintendents that the amount and quality of PLC activity is associated with improved student achievement.[12]

In Windsor, after adopting a districtwide approach to literacy, Feser caused the creation of "data teams" in all of the schools. Osborne in South Orange and Maplewood promoted the use of PLCs as central to their district's "leadership initiative." Zurvalec in Farmington relied on PLCs to implement a "quality instruction initiative." The Farmington PLCs developed rubrics to assess their own growth as learning communities, using the results to spur improvements in instruction and student assessment. Initially, the PLCs focused on student data, typically formative test results as well as state test scores; they later paid increased attention to the assessment of instructional procedures designed to improve student achievement.

In a different move directed toward distributed leadership—in this case, administrators—both Hardy Murphy and Feser participated in the use of instructional rounds, in which principals visited one another's schools to observe and discuss a variety of instructional procedures, some of which they could then adopt in their own schools.[13] Feser was involved in a similar set of rounds with a network of other superintendents drawn together by the Harvard Graduate School of Education's Richard Elmore.

Both the PLCs and instructional rounds are intended to gather principals, superintendents, and teachers into communities of practice focused on instruction; to deprivatize work on instruction and allowing it to be shared across classrooms, schools, and school districts; and to permit certain undiscussables, particularly those related to practices that impede equity, to be confronted. Such a process is expected to disrupt the status quo, replacing it with positive changes in governing variables that increase organizational learning. Thus, in a recursive manner, organizational learning generates teacher and administrator collaboration as an intervention to address achievement gaps, and the intervention further enhances organizational learning.

EXPECTATIONS AND RIGOROUS ACADEMIC EXPERIENCES

The reason given by Osborne for why achievement gaps were so pernicious and persistent was: "Expectations, expectations, expectations!" One set of expectations perpetuating gaps in achievement, according to a number of superintendents, inhered in teachers' beliefs regarding the immutability of student capability and the resulting expectation that certain students would fail if provided rigorous academic experiences. Typically, therefore, teachers across the districts at first tended to resist attempts to increase the number and proportion of students engaged in rigorous academic experiences, expecting the results of such efforts to lower standards. But the experience of most of the districts that moved in that direction proved the opposite was true. For example, (as noted in chapter 1) involving all elementary students in rigorous academic experiences by eliminating the amount of ability or achievement grouping in reading and mathematics instruction resulted in improved performance across the entire population. Similarly, removing the barriers to entry to advanced classes in middle and high school and increasing the proportion of students of color in those classes did not increase the failure rates in advanced classes such as grades 7 or 8 algebra and geometry, and there was no decrease in the proportion of high school students earning 3s on AP exams or 4s on IB exams (the scores most colleges and universities recognize for college credit).

Mark Freeman's approach had simply been to announce that the prerequisites, including teacher recommendations, for Shaker Heights AP and honors classes would be abolished. While greeted with considerable dismay and concern, the elimination of prerequisites stood and student achievement on balance appeared not to suffer from expanding access and enrollment. Sue Zurvalec recounted that sometime around 2008, Farmington had removed the prerequisites for enrollment in AP courses. Three years later, African American student enrollment in advanced classes tripled. She mentioned, in addition, that the AP scores were stable and the district was launching the development of an IB magnet school to further increase the enrollment of students of color in academically demanding classes.

A number of years before Zurvalec's initiative, the Arlington schools also abolished the barriers and prerequisites to student enrollment in accelerated, AP and IB classes; aggressively recruited students of color identified as likely to be successful in such classes; and allowed other students who wished to enroll to do so. The proportion of students of color engaged in AP and IB classes more than doubled, without a corresponding decline in AP scores. By 2009, approximately three out of every four graduates across the Arlington high schools had taken one or more AP or IB classes. As was the case in Farmington, Shaker Heights, and in a number of other districts, Arlington teachers were initially resistant. However, when they understood that there was no pressure to lower class standards, that positive steps were being taken to support the new advanced students, and that professional development would be provided, teacher talk changed from concerns about lower outcomes to sharing information about how to ensure the success of students new to rigorous instruction.[14]

In terms of professional development, teachers of advanced classes in all districts participated in programs and workshops that coached them about ways to deliver the revised instruction and to deal with the changed composition of their classes. Development included external training for high school teachers in AP and IB instruction. The major professional development in this work was situated, as Knapp had envisioned (see quote at the beginning of this chapter), within the professional practice itself.[15] Teachers by necessity adjusted their instruction and, as a result of their own positive experiences and those of their colleagues, revised their expectations of the students who could be successful in their classes and took pride in their ability to support students new to academic rigor.

Opening access to more advanced curricula and courses was not done in isolation. The pattern was typically to spotlight a more comprehensive strategy to support students academically *and* affectively.

CONFRONTING RACE

As we have noted, the programs were aimed not only at supporting student achievement, but also helping students previously excluded from challenging experiences to feel that their minority identities were not a limiting factor. Given MSAN's emphasis on closing gaps between white students and students of color, it is no surprise that almost all of the superintendents tackled the issue of race. There was little doubt that institutional racism and white privilege played a role in perpetuating the correlation between race and student achievement, although given the profile of their districts, overt, intentional racism was relatively uncommon. Since MSAN's founding in 1999, all member districts have been engaged in training of one sort or another related to race. A popular approach has been using the direct services and/or materials provided by Glenn Singleton, a private consultant who specializes in what he calls *courageous conversations*. His book of the same name provides a framework for understanding racism and for confronting beliefs about race through dialogue. In defining courageous conversations, Singleton characterizes them as a kind of dialogue or "strategy for deinstitutionalizing racism and improving student achievement" focused on answering three questions: "Why do racial gaps exist? What is the origin of the racial gaps? What factors have allowed these gaps to persist for so many years?"[16]

Several of the book's examples are based on Singleton's experiences in the Chapel Hill-Carrboro City Schools under the leadership of Neil Pederson.[17] When Pederson first introduced difficult discussions about race more than a decade ago he found that because such conversations had never taken place in the district before, the way forward in the first two years was "rockiest." Elaborating on the troubled beginning, Pederson commented:

> The white teachers largely felt like they were being blamed, that they were being made to feel guilty, that they were even . . . feeling like they were being called racists . . . African American teachers—of course, I'm generalizing here . . . —many of them felt like, "We've had these conversations before, they're painful, and they don't get us anywhere. And I'm tired of telling white folks . . . what it's like. They don't really listen to us. And we're just wasting our breath and I'd rather not go through this again."

Pederson brought in external consultants to open up conversation and provide training on addressing the issue. Ten years later, the Chapel Hill-Carrboro City teachers no longer felt as they did in the beginning. They were supportive and appreciative of the training and its effects, and it seemed as though what had been learned about racism and white privilege had been institutionalized. The training became routine and was eventually conducted internally, as opposed to being provided by external consultants, which helped induce a greater level of comfort. Although he said he could not point to a one-to-one relationship between these conversations and any particular changes in practice, Pedersen did believe that conducting the conversations was as or more important than changes in programs and the allocation of resources to bring about greater equity:

> I guess I would say that in the last ten years, the most courageous parts [of what we have done to advance equity] have been . . . dealing with race and racism and white privilege, and those terms that make people uncomfortable. It's not really courageous to allocate some more resources to fill gaps and services we should be providing for students. It's [important] to be able to see where they are and identify them and advocate for them, but I wouldn't call that courageous particularly. But dealing with this country's racial history and our own personal racial biographies, as we call them, is challenging work.

In line with MSAN's commitment to cultural competence in Arlington, Pat Murphy and his school board continued and extended the districtwide cultural competence development initiated in the three or four years before he became superintendent. That work began with all administrators attending a daylong workshop with Glenn Singleton, followed by the development of a plan to have all faculty and staff help design and participate in cultural competence training. The first year of cultural competence work involved regularly scheduled discussions between administrators, in groups of ten to twelve, confronting issues of race and privilege. Each group was facilitated by two other members of the administrative staff. The facilitators also met as a separate group to debrief and plan succeeding small group sessions. Simultaneously, selected teachers and specialists were trained to conduct cultural competence sessions for all faculty and staff, and a plan was developed to conduct the training school by school over a period of years.[18] That training was still in progress in 2012 and had been extended to the school board which was conducting its own conversations about race with Murphy and with one another, with the assistance of two external facilitators.

Professional development to confront race seems to be another way of working on the issue of expectations, particularly those directed toward students of color, and students who are poor, or speak a first language other than English. The superintendents who spoke about expectations recognized that racism might be driving the achievement gap but believed that most of their (predominantly white) teachers did not display overt racism. Instead, they saw staff as having expectations—which in many cases might have been the consequence of unconscious bias based on their own racial development—that caused them to communicate lower expectations without either intending or realizing it.

Even superintendents sensitive to issues of race were not immune to unconscious biases. The issue was addressed in early MSAN governing board discussions, stimulated in large part by an article about "racial microaggressions" ranging from overt and intended racism to unintended microaggressions. Two cited examples of unintended microaggressions involved assuming Latino American or Asian American students born in the United States were foreign-born by saying "you speak good English," sending a message that the student is an "other"; or proclaiming to a person of color that "everyone can succeed in this society if they try hard enough," thus denying the role of race in determining success in our society.[19] As a former member of the governing board, Smith remembers reading the article for the first time and being nonplussed to recognize himself in at least a few of the examples cited there. He frequently refers to the article when conducting workshops and defies white audience members to read the examples and not to see themselves in at least one or two of them.

CONCLUSION

It seems natural that superintendents intent on realizing greater opportunity for all students on equitable terms would see professional development as a key tool. It seems equally apparent that professional development in the service of equity needs to address increasing the capacity of teachers to implement rigorous curricula for all students; give teachers new or improved instructional skills for differentiating their treatment of students who have different needs and backgrounds; help teachers communicate consistently high expectations for student performance; and mitigate the effects of institutionalized racism and unconscious bias. Yet addressing these needs is neither simple nor easy.

Different superintendents working in different contexts with different faculties used various means to accomplish the same general goal, but most of their professional development strategies included elements of each of the approaches described in this chapter: consistency in expectations in what is taught, how it is taught, and how it is measured; rigorous academic experiences available and promoted for all students; teacher collaboration directed toward increased student performance; implementation of equitable curriculum and instruction through vehicles such as professional learning communities; and a drive for high expectations and confronting issues of race and privilege directly and openly.

With curricular coherence and enhanced professional development as a strong foundation, the superintendents focused their attention on expanding opportunities for previously underserved students and rallied their forces to create equitable opportunities to shrink achievement gaps. Chapter 6 illustrates how they did so.

CHAPTER SIX

Creating Opportunities to Advance Equity

We described in chapter 5 how superintendents employed professional development as a gap-closing strategy internal to the school district, and especially professional development as one of several means by which superintendents address factors over which they have greater influence. In this chapter, we also address opportunities outside of the school, such as initiatives related to jobs, increased income, adequate housing, or provision of better public health service—conditions not susceptible to change based on augmented teacher capacity—that may have an equal bearing on achievement gaps. In addition, we explore the issue of the relationship between opportunity and achievement gaps and the degree to which schools can address either or both of them.

THE CONVERSATION ABOUT OPPORTUNITY GAPS

Most of the superintendents recognized the importance of out-of-school factors in creating and perpetuating gaps in opportunities and achievement, and engaged in discussions regarding the degree to which they should be addressed. Some believed, along with many scholars, that the school exerts a somewhat limited impact on achievement outcomes, but they also felt it was important *not* to talk about that with faculty and community members.

Brookline's Bill Lupini echoed the sentiments of several of his colleagues about how to respond to those members of the faculty and staff, board, and community who ask whether the school can actually make a difference in closing gaps caused by out-of-school factors:

> I tell them that's an interesting conversation and it's one we should have. But part of the problem I think we've had over the past seven years, and I saw it initially, is that tended to be used as an excuse. We probably haven't had that conversation terribly often because . . . I've always worried about where it goes. And where that conversation tends to go is saying we can't be held responsible, and I just think that's garbage.

Speaking openly about the importance of factors such as income, housing patterns, and the racial, language, and income composition of the school in predicting and determining achievement gaps might "let the schools off the hook"—provide excuses for not making progress and thus result in inattention to and inaction in tackling the inequities that schools could and should resolve.

On the other hand, a number of scholars strongly advocate for openly addressing out-of-school factors. Welner and Carter, for example, suggest that a focus on achievement gaps represents a "misguided and mishandled" approach by spotlighting the achievement results rather than the conditions—the opportunity gaps—that create the achievement gaps.[1] Gloria Ladson-Billings recommends that rather than addressing achievement gaps, educators should pay attention to paying back the "education debt" incurred by years of morally corrupt and discriminatory social and educational policies and funding.[2]

This conflict is not of recent origin. At least as early as 1966, with the publication of James Coleman and colleagues' seminal study *Equality of Educational Opportunity*, there have been arguments regarding the degree to which in-school factors could explain differences in achievement. Coleman et al. suggested that educational inputs such as per-pupil expenditures and teachers' level of education, could explain only 10 percent of the variance in achievement across all students and 20 percent for minority students. Out-of-school factors, particularly socioeconomic status, explained much more of the variance.[3] This and additional studies, such as those conducted by Jencks et al., led many educators to conclude that schools could do little about addressing gaps in learning across social classes and racial/ethnic groups.[4] More recent analyses have reached similar conclusions. Rothstein, for example, suggests that schools were setting themselves up for failure by announcing the goal of eliminating achievement gaps because school factors could not overcome the influence of social class in student achievement, adding that ". . . scholarly efforts over four decades have consistently confirmed Coleman's core finding; no analyst has been able to attribute less than two-thirds of the variation in achievement among schools to the family characteristics of their students."[5] Berliner's recent essay argues against the testing regimen of NCLB and its provisions that hold schools responsible for removing gaps in education, when ". . . school effects account for about 20 percent of the variation in achievement test scores . . ." compared with out-of-school variables, which ". . . account for about 60 percent of the variance that can be accounted for in student achievement."[6]

In *Our Kids: The American Dream in Crisis*, Putnam expresses much the same view. He answers the question: "Do K–12 schools make the opportunity gap better or make it worse?" by saying:

> [T]he gap is created more by what happens to kids before they get to school, by things that happen outside of school, and by what kids bring (or don't bring) with them to school . . . than by what schools do to them. The American public school today is as a kind of echo chamber in which the advantages or disadvantages that children bring with them to school have effects on other kids.

But Putnam further states, "We've seen evidence that schools . . . sometimes modestly contribute to leveling the playing field." He reaches a conclusion that would have been a helpful and hopeful point of departure for the MSAN superintendents' discussions where opinions regarding the impact and role of the school ranged from the "no excuses" variety in which schools were fully responsible for eradicating achievement gaps to despair that schools could do anything about such gaps in the face of the power of poverty in determining achievement:

> The fact that schools as an organization today have a mixed and modest impact on the opportunity gap does not mean that reforms in schools might

not be an important part of the solution to the gap. On the contrary, even if schools didn't cause the growing opportunity gap—and there's little evidence that they have—they might well be a prime place to fix it.[7]

We believe most of the MSAN superintendents would likely agree with Putnam that the schools are *an* appropriate place to address opportunity gaps, but certainly not *the* only or even the most important place. Although they were apprehensive that discussing the role of out-of-school factors might incur backlash or stymie efforts to close achievement gaps within schools, all of them appeared to be committed to doing so in order to bring about change in their districts. Neil Pederson in Chapel Hill-Carrboro City expanded on this:

> When we're trying to level the playing field, I think society keeps making it less and less level. I think it's unrealistic to think that doesn't make any difference. And to a great extent that inequity still has significant racial overtones to it. But that's not the speech that I give as superintendent. The other perspective that I give is that society is what it is, family structures are what they are, backgrounds that children bring to school are different, but we as a school system have limited impact on those influences. We know from the literature that there are hundreds of cases of students at schools that have defied those odds for students who don't have those advantages [and nevertheless] are successful in school in large numbers. Our job as educators is to educate every student who comes through the doors, and if some students have less of a support system than others, then we need to provide them a greater support system within our schools. And that's the way we can do our part in leveling the playing field. I think that we can set high standards that we want to achieve and that we must and can . . . assume the responsibility for being totally committed to all students meeting those standards.

Notwithstanding the powerful influences of out-of-school factors in determining educational outcomes, all of the superintendents believed that the schools were, in fact, responsible for at least a portion of the gaps in achievement and were capable of mediating the negative effects of some of those out-of-school factors. As Smith reflected about his Arlington schools experiences, we can acknowledge that school factors may currently be responsible for explaining only 10–40 percent of the variance in measured educational achievement (depending on the measures and method employed, and the time of the study), but there is no reason to believe that percentage represents a fixed ceiling. Perhaps, given greater attention to the issue and more effective interventions, schools can exert a greater impact.[8] Thus, superintendents and all district personnel looked for and created opportunities to respond meaningfully to out-of-school factors by leveraging what they were capable of changing within their systems.

CREATING OPPORTUNITIES

As we looked at the opportunities for achievement the MSAN superintendents labored to establish in their districts, we were struck by both the similarities in the nature of the opportunities they developed and the differences in approaches and emphases. In a few instances, we noted how their moves to create opportunities were similar to those recommended by a number of scholars writing on the limited nature of schools' ability to respond to opportunity gaps.[9] The opportunities created in the MSAN districts included in-school interventions designed to (1) expand early childhood experiences, (2) augment access to rigorous schoolwork and superior instruction, (3) provide culturally responsive curriculum and instruction, and (4) prepare students for early college experiences. In addition, superintendents created conditions to improve opportunities related to out-of-school factors through collaboration with community organizations. We turn now to the strategies they used to provide each of these opportunities.

Early Childhood Intervention

Several of the scholars who have written about the importance of out-of-school factors in creating and perpetuating gaps in educational opportunities and achievement identify the provision of early childhood education for all families as a critical factor in closing gaps that are evident when children first come to school.[10] Several of the superintendents made the same argument and made efforts to establish and/or expand early childhood education. For example, Betty Feser and Brian Osborne focused on completing the implementation of full-day kindergarten as a lever to close an important opportunity gap; Dan Nerad and Judy Wilson created equitable opportunities by expanding pre-K education.

We found it curious that so few superintendents mentioned early childhood initiatives in our interviews, given the number of states that have launched pre-K programs in recent years and reports in the literature attesting to their long-lasting effects on educational attainment; positive health and social outcomes; and return on investment, largely through savings on future expenditures in special education, remedial education, health care social services, and incarceration.[11] It might be that in most of these districts, early childhood initiatives had been implemented before the time of the interviews and greater attention was being paid to other concerns. In Arlington, for example, implementation of full-day kindergarten, an early initiative of work on the achievement gap, had been accomplished in the late 1990s, and the attention on early childhood had turned to leveling opportunities for families to have their children participate in pre-K. By 2009, virtually all families that could qualify for free and reduced-price lunch had access to free pre-K services for their four-year-olds through the public schools, and many of their three-year olds, through the public schools or Head Start. Thus, it is unsurprising that Pat Murphy did not mention early childhood as an initiative on which he was focused. Similarly, early childhood initiatives were old news for Bill Lupini. Brookline is the home the Brookline Early Education Project (BEEP), of one of the best-known research sites for early intervention. BEEP conducted a follow-up study of participating students at age twenty-five, and found that children who had received BEEP services, particularly the disadvantaged students, had more social advantages than those who had not been in the program. Unusual at the time of its inception, BEEP was operated by the public schools.[12]

Feser, whose district had no early childhood program when she took up her role, tenaciously pursued bringing full-time kindergarten to Windsor. Until that time, efforts to start full-day kindergarten had been frustrated by absence of the classroom space it would require and tepid support from the school board. Yet the evening before speaking to us, Feser had attended the first parent forum on a plan to create a full-day kindergarten program that would be consolidated in four schools where space would be made available through revision of the geographic attendance boundaries that determine which schools students will attend.

Like Feser, Osborne entered a school district that offered only half-day kindergarten. In his third year in South Orange and Maplewood, he succeeded in implementing full-day kindergarten as part of the LEARNS (an acronym for *L*eadership, *E*valuation, *A*ccess, *R*igor, a*N*alysis, and *S*upport) plan he and the board fashioned. The elements of LEARNS represented what Osborne identified as his theory of action, which when fulfilled would result in every graduating senior's being able to choose to go to, and be successful in, a four-year college. Osborne promoted full-day kindergarten, which fell under the "Access" label, as a major step toward that end. The initiative necessitated finding an additional $1.5 million in resources, which under the system in New Jersey required that the school district conduct a special election to raise the money from taxpayers. The voters approved.

Clearly proud of the program's success, Osborne commented on the early response to the initiative from first-grade teachers, his board, and the community, who all recognized the importance to later success of creating a more level playing field from the onset of school experiences:

> And what the first-grade teachers told us, and you've heard this a million times . . . was that there are kids who have half-day and their parents pay for great programs [for the second half of the day] and they're completely ready for first grade, and then there are kids who have half-day and then they go to day care and sit in front of a television set and they're a disaster when they get to first grade. So, there's no group happier with full-day kindergarten than our first-grade teachers. That's been a big thing [in expanding access to quality early childhood experiences and narrowing initial gaps in achievement].

In Princeton, the other New Jersey district, a special election also brought an expansion of early childhood services. Unlike South Orange and Maplewood where the issue was full-day kindergarten, the issue here was providing all children with pre-K experiences. The program was initially funded as part of a $2.5 million voter-approved referendum that included pre-K services as well as an expansion of other supplemental services (e.g., additional guidance counselors and extended day activities) designed to reduce gaps in opportunities. Thus these activities became part of school funding and did not disturb the funding of programs already in place. According to Wilson, that was a significant feature in ensuring the "overwhelming approval" of the initiative and helped ensure its expansion from half-day to full-day pre-K services:

> There had been no pre-K for children of poverty. That was a huge and successful piece of our work in my seven years [as superintendent]. It started out as half-time, but the last three years it's been full-time, and it's been very, very influential and productive in terms of how we've made progress with . . . children of early childhood age.

Dan Nerad headed a similar drive for pre-K service expansion in Madison. He identified the rapid expansion of pre-K services for unserved four-year-olds as a major accomplishment in creating opportunities and closing gaps:

> I'm very proud that we've been able to establish . . . beginning this fall, a four-year-old kindergarten program. We have eighteen hundred age-eligible kids, and within three days we had twelve hundred of them signed up, and now there are fourteen hundred . . . signed up already . . . There's high-quality early learning in this community because of the university. And the city has separate accrediting standards for child-care centers. But what is not available here is universal access. So we will now have created that universal access for four-year-olds here.

Considering the responses of Nerad and the other three superintendents who were at the time heavily engaged in the expansion of early childhood opportunities and the accomplishments of other communities which had already moved through a process of expanding such services, it is apparent that early childhood education was seen as a major force in narrowing gaps in opportunities and, as a consequence, in achievement. These superintendents used what they knew of early childhood research and the experiences of their primary-grades teachers to expand the reach of their systems to three- to five-year-olds. This is an important shift in the norms, or governing variables, of the school district's responsibility, and the superintendents felt vindicated in this effort by positive achievement results.

Access to Rigor and Excellence in Instruction

Expanding access to rigorous and high-quality instruction was another key intervention for narrowing gaps in achievement. Many of the strategies used to increase such access were shared across districts, some more universally than others; some strategies were employed by only one or two districts.

One of the most common strategies applied at the elementary level was to shrink or abolish the practice of pulling selected students out of the classroom for special program services. Many scholars and practitioners view this practice as creating conditions of *instructional incoherence.* In this view, instructional coherence is eroded when children, especially those with special needs, are subjected to separate and sometimes conflicting instructional approaches and curriculum provided by a different teacher. This is especially true when the alternative instruction is less rigorous than that occurring in the regular classroom. The practice also prevents such children's access to the full curriculum provided by the classroom teacher.[13] The different curricula with different expectations thus deny the selected students time with their classroom teacher and render their instructional experience less consistent and rich. Not surprisingly, students who have been withheld from the regular curriculum for special instruction—for example, remediation or mastery of "prerequisite skills"—tend to perform less well on that curriculum.[14] The students most frequently singled out for such treatment in the MSAN districts tended to be youngsters identified for special education, English language instruction, and/or remedial education. They also tended to be disproportionately students of color.

Typically, the superintendents' drive to achieve instructional coherence by decreasing or discontinuing the practice of sending students out of the classroom appeared to be connected to the strategy discussed in chapter 5 of creating a school system, instead of a system of separate schools and classrooms, through the creation of a systemwide curriculum and set of instructional procedures. As noted in chapter 3, after emphasizing common goals across schools, Hardy Murphy in Evanston-Skokie made it a priority to halt the practice of sending students to separate instruction and leaving a relatively small number of largely white children to receive regular reading instruction.

Princeton, in addition to discontinuing the procedure of sending students out of the classroom within the school, engaged in decreasing the number of students sent out of the district for special or remedial instruction. Wilson identified moving toward greater inclusion as a critical change in how Princeton treated its instructional organization.

> One of the biggest cultural shifts is probably inclusion work where children are not pulled out of classrooms. We do a lot of co-teaching. Our entire middle school is based on co-teaching now. We've brought low special education programs back into the district for reasons of inclusion. We've added programs every year to the district.

These strategies appeared in secondary schools as well, particularly in initiatives to ensure that English language learners and special education students received content instruction from well-prepared teachers. These teachers who were trained in special education or ESOL were not always prepared or qualified to teach the subjects in which support was needed. This problem was particularly acute in mathematics and science.

Secondary schools, and especially high schools, also had strategies related to changing the bureaucratic procedures for how students might access more rigorous instruction. In addition to arranging for or providing professional development to prepare teachers to work with students previously excluded from AP, honors, or IB classes, superintendents changed the ways in which students could be placed in classes, reorganized the structure or leveling of classes, and created additional support for the previously ineligible students. The ways in which these changes occurred varied, as did the supports put in place to help students engage in rigorous courses.

Mark Freeman addressed access in Shaker Heights by announcing that students and their parents could make the decision as to whether to enroll in advanced classes and that the previous set of prerequisites based on grades and teacher recommendations would be set aside.

In Arlington, after considerable discussion and debate among teachers, staff, and parents, a relatively complex set of prerequisites and approval procedures was abandoned and promising students of color were identified and recruited to enroll in rigorous courses such as geometry and Algebra 1 in middle school and AP and IB classes in high school. Depending on the school, students were identified and recruited in a variety of ways. For example, in some cases teachers identified students whom they believed might be successful in and benefit by taking an advanced class; principals would then have face-to-face meetings with these students and invite them to enroll. In a variation of this process, students were identified by PSAT scores, which were predictive of success in advanced placement classes.[15]

Pat Murphy reflected on Arlington's work in encouraging students to enroll in advanced classes and the concerns this raised about pushing youngsters too fast and hard. He made it clear that instead of creating barriers to enrollment of students in advanced classes (as was the case fifteen years ago, when Smith took on the superintendency), it was now the role of the schools to encourage and support such ambitions;

> We have conversations here about our aspirations for kids, or what our goals and missions are. Some of our community gets a little annoyed with that. That might be the best way [to express that]. "You're pushing kids. You're just worried about numbers." . . . I do say to the community, "Those are my responsibilities in my role . . . At the end of the day, your decision making will always trump my decision making. So, if you don't want your kids in advanced classes, or you don't want your children to do that because you feel it's not the right experience or there's too much pressure, that's your decision. The same is true if you want your child in a particular advanced class. We'll give you advice about that. But if you want them in that class, they'll go in that class and we'll support them."

Easing restrictions and increasing recruitment were often joined by changes in the structure of course offerings in which multiple "ability" or "achievement" levels of classes within each major subject were compressed into either AP or IB and regular offerings.[16] Osborne faced considerable controversy in South Orange and Maplewood when ability levels were compressed in both elementary and secondary schools and requirements to enroll in advanced high school classes were eased:

It's just incredible to me how such a deep blue, politically liberal place where people go for diversity like South Orange and Maplewood can spend so much energy judging, labeling, and sorting the kids. There's just so many ways it happens. I'm still trying to figure out all the ways that it happens in our little system after the three years . . . we've been able to make structural changes. They've been very contentious. You know, they've filled the auditorium until four o'clock in the morning on board meeting nights when we've gotten approval.

As Pat Murphy noted, along with changing the process by which students are allowed to enroll in advanced classes and altering the structure of classes—or *detracking*—it was important that students new to the advanced classes received support in becoming successful. Such supports manifested in a variety of ways, including peer support groups, summer experiences before entering advanced classes in the fall, booster classes offered in conjunction with local universities (more on this below), supplemental classes or seminars, and extended day assistance during the school year.

One example of peer support for academic rigor and excellence in which MSAN districts participated was the annual student conference offered by MSAN itself. It provided what appeared to be a valued support group for high-performing students of color selected by participating districts.

Arlington's Wakefield High School cohort group, which was formed in 1999 and continues today, represents another example of an approach that was widely shared across the MSAN districts. The program identified promising male freshmen of color, who then met in a weekly session moderated by two or three staff members with the purpose of working through issues experienced in entering and becoming successful in advanced classes. When this approach began, fifteen students were represented in twenty-one AP classes. By 2008–2009, eighty-five students in the cohort were taking 161 AP courses. Black students, representing 29 percent of the school's enrollment, made up about 20 percent of the AP enrollment. Latino students, constituting 44 percent of the school's enrollment, were 40 percent of the AP enrollment.[17]

In addition to peer support, several of the MSAN districts offered AVID classes to help prepare students to be successful in challenging classes. Some districts also provided other supplemental courses, such as the Leadership Class developed in Farmington by student representatives from each of the three Farmington high schools, assisted by graduate students from The University of Michigan. Building on learning about the importance of student voice from their MSAN student conference experiences, the Farmington students, according to Sue Zurvalec, "really talk about the issues of race, stereotyping, discrimination, intervention and about how you peer-to-peer change your school culture." Zurvalec went on to explain:

> They get an elective credit . . . [T]he teacher . . . co-facilitates with the students who have been through the facilitation training and have done the [leadership] class before. So we have upperclassmen who are taking it as a student for the second time, but to help co-facilitate [help the teacher by leading activities] . . . and from my own personal background and love, I said, "I can make this happen. You know, I can help it grow." And it's really become quite amazing . . . I'm really proud of it. I'm proud of the kids because they have embraced it so much.

Providing universal access to the core curriculum at the elementary level, opening access to advanced curricula at the secondary level, and providing affective support that gives young people the confidence and motivation to persist through rigorous classroom experiences is critical to overcoming background differences and narrowing achievement gaps based on demographic characteristics. But keeping students consistently engaged through high school graduation requires attention to cultural differences between home and school that often challenge students in ways unseen by teachers and principals.

Culturally Responsive Curriculum and Instruction

In addition to working on issues of expectations, the Farmington Leadership Class also represents what might be termed an aspect of culturally responsive curriculum and instruction, which appeared to be another strategy of importance to MSAN superintendents. Geneva Gay, a leader for over forty years in developing and explaining culturally responsive teaching, defines it in a 2013 reflective essay on her own work:

Culturally responsive teaching is a technique for improving the performance of underachieving ethnically and racially diverse students. In the United States these students are primarily of Asian, African, Native, and Latino American ancestry, live in poverty, and attend schools in urban and rural areas. This approach to teaching helps all students acquire more knowledge about cultural diversity, and uses the cultural heritages, experiences and perspectives of ethnically diverse students as instructional resources to improve their learning opportunities and outcomes. Thus, it teaches to and through cultural diversity.[18]

We knew from Smith's participation in MSAN governing board meetings that most of the superintendents were interested in culturally responsive teaching, but examples of how it played out in particular classes did not arise frequently in our interviews. Nevertheless, much of the work in which superintendents engaged to confront issues of cultural competence among teachers, administrators, and community members surfaced in most interviews, and that we described earlier, was fueled by their expectation that increased cultural competence would lead to more culturally responsive instruction. One example of focusing on the strategy of culturally responsive teaching—is represented in Jere Hochman's work in Bedford. While lamenting the absence of a plan to correct the underrepresentation of students of color in AP classes in his district and professing intent to increase the presence of more multicultural materials supporting the curriculum, Hochman nevertheless took heart from and was enthusiastic about the activities of what he called the MSAN kids, students who had planned and hosted the annual MSAN student conference in Bedford in 2011 and had adopted an action plan to close achievement gaps. As part of that plan, they conducted a survey to discover teachers' perspectives on proportionate representation by race and ethnicity in AP classes. In Hochman's words,

> One of the questions they . . . want to ask every faculty member [is]: "Do you believe that AP classes should be representative of the . . . demographics of the population of the school district?" And, "Do you believe that there . . . should be more students of color in AP classes?" . . . Now they also have the question that says: "Do you think these classes *could* be representative?" which is a very different question. So they and we are all very eager to see what kind of response we get on that expectation level.

CREATING OPPORTUNITIES TO ADVANCE EQUITY   121

College Preparation

Closely related to efforts to increase access to rigorous curriculum and instruction and to the emphasis on culturally responsive instruction are initiatives to create conditions that motivate students to seek a college education. In addition to ensuring access to rigorous course work, some superintendents implemented a variety of measures intended to help students gain admission and perform successfully in college. Four of the superintendents stood out for their initiatives focused on college attendance, ranging from tracking student progress from middle school to college to providing experiences on college campuses.

Betty Feser used changes in college-going rates for African American students as one of the metrics she followed to determine Windsor's degree of success in opening opportunities and narrowing achievement gaps. Looking back on her ten-year superintendency there, she saw a sea change in perceptions regarding who should be preparing for what kinds of post–high school experiences. She met resistance when she first encouraged staff to change their high school course catalogues to focus on college readiness and not to assume that most students were preparing for work, the military, or trade school, but the effort was successful. Feser reported seeing more impressive progress on the college attendance data than on the state test results:

> Higher percentages of kids of color are going to better colleges. [For example, the] University of Connecticut . . . has risen dramatically in its caliber [and] it's astounding to see the number of kids of color who are now getting accepted. . . . We're seeing [positive] indicators on that and more so than we are in the state testing . . . I can look at the college performance and feel like, "All right, we turned a corner there."

Motivated by a concern similar to Feser's—a pronounced gap in college persistence between black and white students—Brian Osborne described years of concentrated efforts in South Orange and Maplewood to investigate the relationship between middle school course-taking and persistence in college before his arrival in the district. Osborne and his board succeeded in compressing some of the levels of middle school courses based on findings regarding the relationship between middle school course-taking and college persistence. Using National Clearing House research data, which tracks the colleges and universities attended and college completion rates of students from participating districts and schools, Osborne and his staff saw that white youngsters graduating from the school system earned a much higher proportion of college degrees within five years of graduation than black graduates. They also discovered a very strong association between the rigor of middle school and high school classes taken and the likelihood of going to and continuing in college.[19] Sharing those kinds of data with faculty and community (an important component of organizational learning), had been "a huge factor in increasing access."

Judy Wilson in Princeton told of her Generation One program, a concentrated effort to prepare students who, if successful, would be the first in their families to attend college:

> We work with their families, their parents. We educate their parents about what an SAT is, what a FAFSA form is, what a college tour is. We take them on tours. Anyway, we walk them through four-plus years to the graduation line with a college acceptance plan in place. It's very individualized. It might be fifteen to twenty students a year, but with a really high success rate. More than half of them are going to go to exceptional schools that they probably had no idea about.

The Princeton schools partnered with Princeton University to educate families about the college preparation, financing, and admissions processes; provided tutoring and mentoring services beginning in middle school; and conducted social gatherings and special events designed to make the families comfortable with the idea that college attendance was both feasible and desirable.

For over twenty years, the Arlington Public Schools has participated in a program similar to the Generation One initiative. The Early Identification Program operated by George Mason University with Arlington and six other northern Virginia school districts targets likely first-generation college attendees, identifying them in grade 8. These students participate in tutoring with mentors, preparing for college-related tests (e.g., PSAT, SAT), life skills workshops, and a variety of enrichment experiences of-

fered in each school during the school year. Beginning in the summer after grade 9, students attend a three-week Summer Academy on the college
campus, in which they take preparatory or booster classes that set them
up for the advanced classes in which they have enrolled for the following
autumn of grades 10, 11, and 12. A large percentage of these students
enter college at George Mason and other universities, many of them with
full scholarships.[20]

Collaboration with Community Organizations

Recognizing that the schools are unable to mitigate the effects of all out-
of-school factors, some of the superintendents saw collaborative work with
community organizations as an important strategy that cuts across a number of the opportunity gaps on which they were working. Additionally,
they fostered collaborative arrangements in which community organizations helped provide resources for established school district programs
that addressed opportunity gaps.

In Madison, Dan Nerad enthused about creating a partnership with
health-care providers to cover gaps in state insurance coverage for students
who otherwise would have gone without services:

> [T]there is a good recognition here of the outside-of-school factors that affect
> kids' learning. So part of the strategy is a partnership strategy, a collaborative
> strategy. Literally, we don't know how this governor's budget's going [to affect
> health insurance for children]. I mean, we're worried that it may not . . . cover
> as many kids. But, literally, outside of what the state insurance plan picked
> up for low-income kids, there are about two thousand kids within our district
> that couldn't get covered, and we worked in a collaborative with our health-
> care providers to give every kid not covered a health-care home, so they're able
> to go to one of the major providers and have regular appointments.

Nerad made the connection between this accomplishment and Madison's perspectives regarding creating equitable opportunities, indicating
two strands of beliefs:

> [First] . . . a belief that . . . schools can make a difference and we can improve
> our practice, so that's one major strand. And I would say another major strand
> is this piece that we're doing collaboratively with the community.

He described two additional community collaboration efforts. The first was a Schools of Hope program started under the leadership of his predecessor, Art Rainwater, one of the founding MSAN superintendents. Nerad described it as a "comprehensive literacy support program," funded in large part by the United Way, which provided elementary and middle schools with community partner tutors who, along with supplemental literacy instruction, provided drug education. The second was a "one of a kind" extension of the AVID program. Entitled AVID TOPS, it provided mentoring and tutoring through the Boys and Girls Club to first-generation high school students.

Taking the initiative to create health-care options for students in poverty not covered by insurance, involving volunteers from the community to enhance students' literacy, and stretching the highly touted AVID program are three clear examples of taking actions to mitigate opportunity gaps while directly addressing achievement gaps. Health care, literacy, and college-readiness are all linked to a child's circumstances in society—circumstances that are often perceived to be beyond the reach of schools. Nerad demonstrated that such is not necessarily the case.

Lupini described two Brookline collaborative efforts, which like Madison's TOPS program involved community funding of extended programs. The Brookline Education Foundation helped to fund some of the initiatives associated with the state-grant-funded Metco program. Initiated in 1966, Metco is a voluntary busing program intended ". . . to expand educational opportunities, increase diversity, and reduce racial isolation, by permitting students in certain cities to attend public schools in other communities that have agreed to participate."[21] Over three thousand students and over thirty school districts are involved, and Lupini pointed out that Brookline served the second-largest number of students among participating districts. Unlike the Madison example, this effort served students from another community. Lupini also described a program adapted from Arlington that Brookline called the Calculus Project, designed to increase the proportion of students of color in higher-level mathematics. When it was threatened by budget cuts, a local foundation, the Brookline High School 21st Century Fund, offered to help with funding and extending the scope of the program. Thus, Lupini worked with community partners to provide greater access to social capital and rigorous academics that would not naturally occur for the targeted student population.

Coming at the issue from a slightly different direction, Wilson expressed disappointment, despite what she described as "good dialogue," with the degree of collaboration across community organizations and the schools in addressing shared concerns:

> [What] I think [is] frustrating—even in a little town like Princeton—is that there are many, many well-founded, well-intentioned programs that run outside of the schools—afterschool tutoring programs and rec programs and Saturday morning this and Thursday night that. With all those resources and effort and good intentions, I think we could probably do better . . . All these [separate programs]: the health center and the tutoring center four days a week after school, all community-based programs. [If] they could . . . somehow . . . be more closely aligned or under one umbrella, I think we could do better. I think we have the same goal, but what happens at the arts council on Friday afternoon for kids of poverty and what happens Monday through Thursday afternoon . . . You know, they're not well informed about what happens from 8:00 to 3:00. We're not well informed about what's happening, always, from 3:00 to 8:00. Even in our high-level intervention system, where a child needs family interventions or crisis support, sometimes a lot of that gets splintered. This whole idea of wrap-around, we're not good at.

We tend to agree with Wilson that school districts can and should do a better job of coordinating efforts across schools, other agencies and organizations and we believe that is more important than whether an effect is attributable to schools or to out-of-school factors. She and others demonstrate that it may be more effective to think about achievement gaps and opportunity gaps together and to address them with collaborations that cross boundaries between school districts and the communities in which they are embedded.

CONCLUSION

We agree with the superintendents portrayed in this book that schools can't wait for the larger political system to address income, housing, and other gaps before addressing opportunity and achievement gaps in the schools. We also believe, with them, that the schools may not be able to close opportunity and achievement gaps by themselves, but that they can mediate the impact of some of those factors such as income and housing on student achievement. In the following chapter we elaborate this perspective as we describe the ways in which superintendents presented achievement gaps to their organizations and communities. We also portray the threats they faced in pursuing the closing of opportunity and achievement gaps, and the ways in which they parried and mitigated those threats.

CHAPTER SEVEN

Mitigating Threats to an Equity Agenda

The success of initiatives to reduce gaps in opportunities and student learning encountered threats across all of the districts represented in our study. These threats arose from a variety of sources and assumed an array of forms. At the risk of oversimplification, we have elected to use Bolman and Deal's conceptual framework to organize the threats and the behaviors used to deflect or eliminate them. This model suggests four frames through which to analyze organizations: structural, human resource, political, and symbolic. Although for the purposes of this chapter, we organized each threat under a single frame, we recognize that viewing the same phenomena through multiple lenses will enrich our understanding.[1] Thus we discuss each threat and the means of mitigation through one frame, but treat, as appropriate, their relation to other frames.

STRUCTURAL THREATS

Structural threats arise from organizational features that govern the ways in which work is distributed and how it is coordinated. They include roles, goals, policies, plans, rules, procedures, and technology.[2] One clear potential threat to accomplishing the goals of narrowing opportunity and achievement gaps is absence of district agreement to do so. Most of the school districts we have discussed mitigated this threat by generating strong consensus that working on these gaps represented a priority that was reflected in school board strategic plans and in school board policies. As Smith and his colleagues in Arlington indicated, one of the necessary organization conditions for making progress on closing gaps was making it a goal explicitly and repeatedly communicated to staff and community, and supporting this goal through the promulgation of specific objectives and plans, progress on which could be communicated clearly and honestly.[3]

Given MSAN's vision, it is not surprising that the member school districts all placed importance on aligning goals and plans. Even among these similar districts, however, circumstances affected how they circumvented structural threats related to their plans and policies. In Jere Hochman's case, for example, the achievement gap was not necessarily front and center in the Bedford district's plans and goals, unlike his previous district, Amherst-Pelham where the focus on the achievement gap and on equity was "in the DNA" of the district. In fact, a general slogan "excellence in diversity," which Bedford had adopted before his arrival and appeared on the district's web site, seemed to have little or no effect on school district decision making or planning. Rather than focus on the adoption of plans to narrow achievement gaps, Hochman emphasized the importance of ensuring access to high-quality instruction for all students and promoted the ideas that students of all ethnicities and cultures should be able to see themselves in the curriculum and be proportionately represented in all classes and co-curricular activities. In taking this route, Hochman avoided what might have been a contentious issue with his board and faculty—opening up a discussion (and acknowledgment) of the achievement gap—yet found a way to focus on narrowing gaps through instructional avenues designed to broaden opportunities.

More common among these districts was the adoption of strategic plans featuring as a first or second priority the closing of achievement gaps, as was the case in Arlington and Brookline, which we use as representative examples. The superintendents in these districts—Pat Murphy and Bill Lupini, respectively—both had a hand in developing plans that were adopted by their boards and guided them and their staffs. As Murphy described it:

> The strategic plan for the school division . . . began to put those things [objectives and activities designed to eliminate achievement gaps] in place over a decade ago. That was one of the original goals of several plans previous to the one we have today. The plan that we have today also has eliminating the achievement gap as our second goal. The first goal is making sure that all children have challenging and engaging learning experiences.

The plans were seen as critical communications of the relative significance of the work to staff and to the community and served, as well, as an aid to alignment of budget development and allocations and as guidance on the expenditure of staff time. Lupini captured this intent when he said:

> I think our strength is an overall plan. We presented at an MSAN conference in Philadelphia . . . and . . . a number of people . . . said, "Wow! This is the first time we've seen someone come in with a districtwide plan, not a number of initiatives within . . . a school or a set of schools." We really look at everything that we incorporate . . . from professional development through any of these programs under the light of that strategic plan, and in particular this goal number two around the achievement gaps. And if it doesn't meet muster, then it doesn't get funded.

In both of these districts, making the work on the achievement gap the second priority appeared to be a strategy specifically designed to blunt the occasional criticism that students who were represented on the lower side of the gap were taking all of the resources and commitment, and that other students were being ignored. The political and symbolic move of giving highest priority to ensuring positive experiences for all students, as both Murphy and Lupini did, supported the overall structural intent to keep achievement gaps as a high priority while reducing the likelihood of a threat to the continuation of the gap-closing initiatives.

Another common initiative among the districts—allowing greater access to rigorous coursework—was threatened by cumbersome and unnecessary entry requirements for advanced classes. As we have noted, prerequisites for advanced middle and high school courses, and grouping based on achievement or ability assessments in elementary and middle schools tended to impede efforts across most of the districts. Removing or modifying those policies and procedures was a structural strategy many superintendents employed to alleviate this threat to creating opportunities for rigorous instruction for all students, and particularly for those students on the wrong side of the gap.

Similarly, superintendents needed to defuse threats to equal access in the form of policies, procedures, and traditions that restricted opportunities for students of color to engage in certain extra- or co-curricular activities, participate in special events that involved fees or additional costs, or receive awards. Betty Feser, in particular, talked about her concern that in her first years in Windsor, only white students appeared to be receiving awards and recognition at school events in a system in which about 50 percent of the students were African American or Latino. Feser evinced understandable pride in turning that inequity around; as her tenure in Windsor ended, staff members were ensuring that recognition more closely matched the district's student demographics, sending an important symbolic and political message:

> . . . everything I went to when I came into the district, every kid on stage receiving awards [was] white . . . Everybody who was in Advanced Placement was white. Everyone going into National Honor Society was white. That has changed dramatically, and I think . . . there is a mind-set on the part of most staff of starting to recognize that these are all our kids, and our kids are capable. I don't have to say to people anymore that I want [all kids to be represented]. And I had to say it for several years.

In chapter 5, we described the drive by several of the superintendents to work toward changing the structure of the curriculum and modes of instruction to ensure that they were leading a coherent school system. Clearly having every school, or in Hardy Murphy's situation, every teacher, going in a different direction obstructed attempts to provide a single curriculum and to implement common measures of accountability. Dan Nerad reflected on the importance of a consistent curriculum across schools by comparing his experience in Madison to his experience as the superintendent of Green Bay, another MSAN district, in which he spent most of his career:

> One of the things I've come to learn about this district is that it's so decentralized in curriculum and instruction that it's hard to get to a conversation about standards and improving curriculum and instruction across all schools. So I think that's a much different environment than I was in, in Green Bay, where we were much more able to get to the conversation . . .

Feser, Wilson, Lee, Lupini, Osborne, Sherman, and Zurvalec also directly addressed restructuring curriculum and instruction to ensure coordination and consistency across schools and alignment with district goals, helping to increase the chances that equity outcomes will be better aligned with aspirations.

Although professional development represented a major lever to foster consistency and support for systemic goals, many of the superintendents also worked in other ways on ensuring that the leadership in the district in both the central office and among school-based administrators supported the districts' equity initiatives. Methods for maintaining the desired support included structural strategies such as using progress on the goals of strategic plans as a part of personnel evaluation, filling vacancies with administrators sympathetic to the district's goals, increasing the diversity of administrative staff, changing some administrative assignments, and signaling to teachers that they could make changes in the classroom or work somewhere else.

In Farmington, Sue Zurvalec worked with her administrators on creating a common vision, increased the proportion of African American administrators and teachers, encouraged some key retirements, made certain that vacancies were filled by supportive individuals, and made the review of data a feature of her interactions with and evaluation of principals:

> I do visits every week to schools. The first thing I do with the principal is to sit down and say, "So show me what's working. Let's look at the data together." I make that commitment. They know I'm going to look at the data. So, that sends the message. In Michigan, starting this June for principals and next year for teachers, we will have to tie their performance evaluations . . . to

student achievement. So that piece is going to get connected within the next two years.

Mort Sherman in Alexandria pressed hard to change the behaviors of administrators and teachers through presentation of data, encouragement, and evaluation. Those who would not subscribe to the agenda established with the school board were encouraged to find employment elsewhere:

> We have twenty schools . . . Only four principals are here that were here when I came . . . [The changes were made] quietly, methodically. My central office staff—how many were here before? Two.

After Sherman announced plans for changing instruction and procedures at T.C. Williams high school, which had lost its state accreditation and been designated a failing school, seventy of the three hundred high school teachers left the district:

> Teachers across the district got really ticked at me . . . But you know, after I said to them, "Here's who we are as a district, here's how we're going to move forward and you've got to join. You've got to get on board . . ." now they know I'm not kidding . . . They know that we've upped the ante, we've upped the bar. And in order to stay here to work for our kids, because I think it's a privilege to work for these children, you need to improve your game.

Neil Pederson's nineteen-year stint in Chapel Hill-Carrboro City was sufficiently long to allow him to change the district's structure over the course of his tenure. He had hired most of the leaders in the district and believed that their perspectives on equity issues matched his own. Although Bill Lupini's tenure in Brookline was less than half that of Pederson's, he could also comment after seven years that "I've had a chance now to hire all but the headmaster and one elementary principal . . . And we've hired people with a passion for this work."

Thus far, we have described structural threats to the narrowing of opportunity and achievement gaps such as an absence of clear direction, accompanied by organizational arrangements that ensured pursuit of potentially conflicting goals by individual schools and/or departments; a dearth of supporting plans and instructional arrangements; the perpetuation of policies and rules militating against closing gaps in rigorous academic experiences; and personnel in important positions who are resistant to equity goals. To counter these threats, superintendents worked with their boards to develop clear plans and goals, and with their staffs to develop supporting procedures that would ensure that all parts of the organization headed in the same direction. They changed the rules regarding engagement in rigorous academic experiences and moved to place people committed to the work of equity in key positions.

A different kind of structural threat to equity agendas resides in the ways in which budget allocations are made and what they are supposed to achieve. Most of the superintendents talked about the importance of ensuring *equity*—that is, making certain schools and students facing the greatest challenges received the greatest resources—rather than *equality* of expenditures. The way in which budgets get put together may be structural, but dealing with the threats to the end result is clearly political, and we turn to the political response to concerns regarding equitable budgets in the next section.

POLITICAL THREATS

Viewing the work of organizations through the political frame addresses issues such as power, conflict, negotiation, and compromise rooted in the dynamics of divergent interests.[4] Given the diversity of the districts represented in our interviews, we expected to find robust political environments in which different constituencies would struggle over exhaustive resources in pursuit of competing goals.

Except for Paradise Valley, the MSAN districts represented here were well resourced. Yet, even in these relatively wealthy districts, how public funds were spent in schools became of greater concern in the wake of the 2008 recession, which surfaced particular parent groups interested in protecting or expanding programs in which their children were engaged, such as gifted and talented, AP courses, elementary school foreign languages.

Most of these parents tended to be among the more privileged residents of the districts, and most of the superintendents accommodated these groups as a way to guard against losing their focus on equity issues, losing support central to continuing their work, losing their jobs, or losing the patronage of more advantaged families who could afford to enroll their children in private schools.

These constituents were typically in favor of expenditures directed toward equity unless they perceived that their children would be disadvantaged. Mark Freeman, the superintendent with the greatest longevity in one district, described how he and his school boards approached such issues over the years:

> "[I] think that they have dealt with some of the more difficult aspects of this. It's easy to talk about parity and equity and equality, but if you lose the involved, privileged . . . population in a school district, you probably lose the school district. Because sadly, if everybody moves out and you don't have an engaged public, it probably really affects the quality of the school district, community support, [and] the value of criticism . . . I think that people on the Shaker school board have recognized [this fact]. So . . . the directive has always been to do both . . . have a high-quality challenging program for all children, and also deal with these issues of the achievement gap and the human relations aspects . . . I just assume that too. And . . . I think there's been an interest . . . in making sure that the programs are going to be attractive for people that do have more resources.

Toward this end, Freeman had initiated a new K–12 IB program and a new Mandarin language class in 2011 as a way of demonstrating a concern for providing opportunities for people with greater resources, but at the same time making those opportunities available to all.

Like Freeman, Nerad was concerned about serving the more advantaged while maintaining a focus on achievement gaps, under conditions of constricted state funding imposed by Wisconsin's new governor:

> . . . that's where a lot of the strain comes, because there are a lot of people who believe we are not helping sufficiently our advanced learners in the school district. We did a survey of parents who live in our district [but] opted for options other than our district, and [the responses indicated] that we aren't doing enough for talented and gifted kids. And so . . . the message [is that]

we need to improve learning for all kids, and advance achievement for all kids
. . . while we eliminate these achievement gaps.

Lupini shared this balancing approach with Freeman and Nerad. His
strategy was to ensure that programming included initiatives for a variety of interest groups, and thus avoid the perception that some particular
group's ox was gored. Arguing that provision of a program for gifted and
talented students also represents equity, he remarked:

> We do that in a thoughtful way, we don't pull kids out for the gifted and tal-
> ented program. We have grade acceleration, we have subject area acceleration,
> we're about to look at virtual high school. We have opportunities for kids who
> exhaust our courses at the high school to take courses outside, and we reim-
> burse on the Harvard extension rate. And that's one of the ways we keep the
> ox from being gored. [When] people . . . say it's always about X or it's always
> about special education, which we get a lot, we say, "Wait a minute, that's
> not fair . . . How about all the work that's gone into ECS, the Enrichment
> and Challenge Program, around grade acceleration, subject area acceleration,
> reimbursing kids for taking courses at colleges?" . . . I think [these sorts of
> initiatives] . . . allow us to continue the work in Brookline.

Moves to harmonize interests also seemed to come into play in situations in which the families whose children were the target of initiatives to
close opportunity and achievement gaps believed the progress was half-
hearted, too slow, or just wrongheaded. Zurvalec experienced this phenomenon shortly after joining MSAN, when she launched an initiative
designed to support inclusion and diversity in the Farmington schools.
Part of this initiative involved administering Ron Ferguson's Tripod student survey and sharing the results with teachers in the interest of improving teacher-student relationships and the culture of the schools. When
black parents learned of the initiative, rather than thanking the schools for
focusing on the problem, they found the survey inappropriate and were
suspicious of the reasons for using it:

> Our parents, particularly these black parents . . . had moved in from Detroit
> to Farmington Hills. And they believed they had made it; which, in a lot
> of ways they had. They were in a good school system, where their kids were
> learning. But then they found out they still had achievement gaps. And that's

deeply hurtful. And they're saying: "How can this be? We left Detroit and we're here now and this is still going on." So it was a real wake-up call [for us] and it didn't really feel very good. So when we did the Tripod survey, we didn't anticipate the backlash we would get. We thought they . . . would see we're trying to do the right things by asking their students about their perceptions. But instead, they saw this as very intrusive . . . [and asked]: Why haven't you fixed this achievement gap if you knew it was around?

Rather than becoming defensive, Zurvalec and her staff organized a parent forum and invited Ferguson to come and talk with the parents about the Tripod project and its rationale. Although some parents remained angry, many joined with Zurvalec to establish an African American Parent Network, still in operation at the time of the interview, to work on finding solutions to the achievement gap. Zurvalec saw the founding of the parent network as a "turning point" in the school district's relationship with the African American community and attributed its continuation to having established a climate characterized by openness and trust.

We mentioned in chapter 3 a somewhat different development in Alexandria, where Sherman signed a memorandum of understanding with the NAACP and a group representing the Latino community, promising to work with the schools on resolving problems of disproportionality in achievement, discipline, and other matters, rather than "feuding." Before this agreement, the community had historically been skeptical of the school district's commitment to recognizing and acting on the problem of differential achievement and treatment. Sherman found the work that followed the signing of the MOU in Alexandria a force for developing additional allies in the community and a catalyst for progress.

When faced with political threats, superintendents engaged as political actors and sought to create coalitions that would help them preserve their equity agendas. They understood the potential for strife in multifaceted interests and competition over resources. With their school boards as their political bases, they engaged in continuing efforts to keep their communities satisfied and to help them understand both the nature of the effort to mitigate achievement gaps and how all children were being served by their school systems.

HUMAN RESOURCE THREATS

The human resource frame focuses on threats arising from the relationship between employees and the organization, relationships between individuals and groups within the organization, and disagreements between members of the organizations and members of their communities.[5] Human resource threats to the work on opportunity and achievement gaps tended to revolve around cultural competence issues such as teacher expectations for students of color and the role of race and ethnicity among faculty members, among students, and between the organization and the community. Several of the districts confronted these issues directly over a sustained period of time.

One of the earliest and most systematic and prolonged initiatives occurred in Chapel Hill-Carrboro City, beginning with Neil Pederson's collaboration with Glenn Singleton.[6] In that district, the threats to the work on the achievement gap arose from all of the sectors of the organization and its community, including the school board, involved in the initiative. Some school board members questioned the approach of holding courageous conversations about race and achievement during training, advocating instead for a more "color-blind approach, which is antithetical to the approach that we were taking," according to Pederson.

This putative color-blind approach was identified by several superintendents as a barrier or threat to the kind of professional and community development in which districts were engaged. It was typically expressed in assertions such as: "I don't see race or color, I just see kids." Ullicci and Battey, two teacher educators who have worked on this issue (and with whom we agree), suggest that "[w]hile color blindness is generally sold as a positive—that in ignoring color, racism is minimized—we will argue that instead color blindness contributes to a collective ignorance and relieves individuals from fighting against the impact of racism."[7]

The threat to conducting work on cultural competence represented by color-blindness is typically joined by resistance to the concept of white privilege (which, among its other benefits, confers the privilege of not worrying about race or color and not recognizing the privileges extended to those who are white).[8] In *Gaining on the Gap*, Smith et al. describe a number of approaches to addressing such issues with teachers, students, parents, and community members as a way to remove the threats and advance the work on opportunity and achievement gaps. In particular, those who facilitated the training sessions argued the importance of telling personal stories related to race, including white participants, many of whom had not thought about race in relation to themselves; and directly confronting the issues of conveying low expectations and propagating stereotype or identity threats.[9] The issue of stereotype or identity threat was added to cultural competence discussions as Claude Steele and his colleagues and former students' research was shared across the MSAN districts.[10] In Arlington, seminars and workshops were designed, with faculties and administrators of all schools participating in the sessions. Cultural competence seminars for community members have also been offered for over a decade and continue today, and students have been and continue to be involved in similar experiences, including the recent publication of a collection of student poetic reflections on "Black Lives Matter."[11]

Based on our interviews, cultural competence training appeared to be the favored antidote for skewed expectations for students based on race or ethnicity, color-blindness, and denial of white privilege. Paradoxically, however, cultural competence development sessions may themselves represent a threat to continuing the work on closing gaps. As noted in chapter 3, Neil Pederson wondered whether the longevity of district efforts and the difficulty of attributing progress on student learning and expanded opportunities to cultural competence training had created a sense of ennui. He felt there was "pushback in that we've been focusing on this so long, that some . . . are ready for us to move on to something else."

In addition to Pederson's concern, it appears clear from interviews across the superintendents that color blindness and rejection of the concept of white privilege sometimes merge with resentment among white faculty members that their expectations for and behaviors toward students might be interpreted as based on factors other than individual performance, or that inequity in opportunity and achievement might be attributable to institutional racism.

Most of the superintendents believed that institutional racism and white privilege played an important role in perpetuating achievement gaps. But they did not believe the problem was overt racism. Rather, they believed institutional racism and white privilege arose from implicit and unconscious biases manifested in microaggressions, presumed color blindness and other more subtle ways, ranging from textbook selection to favored cultural events. If faculty and community members believe that the professional and community development efforts are focused on curbing overt racism, then the attempt to work on white privilege and racial micro aggressions will likely fail. Mitigating these kinds of human relations threats takes careful planning of professional development, but also requires, we believe, thoughtful analysis through the symbolic frame.

SYMBOLIC THREATS

We have already touched on an array of symbolic threats in different forms. The symbolic frame approaches organization events from the perspective of symbols such as vision, myths, stories, rituals, and ceremonies.[12] If a district's stories, myths, rituals, and ceremonies depict the status quo as positive and working for all students, then that message represents a direct threat to working on equity. That was the dilemma that superintendents in several districts faced: it was difficult to argue for change if the district and the community thought the system was working perfectly well. Moreover, if work on issues of equity is seen as redistributing resources from one group to advantage another, then that conveys a strikingly different message than the idea that working on issues of equity represents a time-honored American ideal of treating all people with respect and creating conditions of equal opportunity. Participating superintendents endeavored to communicate important symbols to deemphasize the former and emphasize the latter.

To discover the ways in which the superintendents attempted to make the enterprise and the message at least palatable to their constituents, we asked how they explained their work on the achievement gap. As we noted in previous chapters, many of the communities represented took pride in their commitment to social justice. Some of the superintendents referenced that commitment explicitly and located their work in that tradition. In the parlance of the symbolic frame, the superintendents employed the stories of racial and socioeconomic integration to explain the equity work they were doing in their school districts.

Freeman recalled his early days as a teacher in Shaker Heights and becoming involved in discussions and the development of plans for evening out disproportionate black-white enrollments in the community's elementary schools. The community was proud of the fact that it had been an early proponent of fair housing and actively promoted integration. Despite that stance, racial housing patterns in the school district, which included a section of the city of Cleveland, were mostly segregated across an east-west line, and the student population of schools located on one or the other side of that line reflected that segregation. As we saw above, Freeman advocated expenditures that would ensure that the community remained diverse (e.g., programming to discourage white flight), but nevertheless was an outspoken advocate for equity with community and faculty members, identifying the improvements in the rigor and breadth of programs as a boon to all students.

Evanston-Skokie's school board also conveyed pride in its commitment to providing equitable programs in its schools, and there was no question that they not only would support Hardy Murphy's intent to work on achievement gaps; they *expected* him to treat elimination of those gaps as a priority. Recognizing that there might be a point at which those committed to equity would balk if they believed their children's opportunities might be curtailed, Murphy adopted a nuanced approach to explaining and justifying his work to the community. Among the superintendents we interviewed, he probably spent the most time talking about his thinking about and treatment of the issue. Murphy had worked on the achievement gap for a number of years (in Texas before coming to Evanston), and described the way he had changed in his thinking and in his public presentations about the achievement gap:

> For many years I tried not to use the term *achievement gap* . . . because I would just talk about excellence for all children. But what I found out was

that at the end of the day, you have to underscore the piece that there's a difference between the way children achieve. My thinking was I did not want to stereotype black children as failures, because many of them are doing very, very well. And actually, we see more doing better over time. But when I talk about the achievement gap, I talk about it as something that has historical roots [reflected in] . . . differences in life opportunities and treatment . . . the differences that have occurred between African Americans and Latinos and others in the country. I don't think there's any other way to talk about it.

Murphy went on to describe how he avoided an adverse reaction to work on opportunity and achievement gaps by exercising caution and avoiding any sense that he was impeaching the motives of community members and teachers:

I think you have to be careful when you talk about it, because you don't want to indict people. I think that, by and large, most people want to do the right thing and want to see all children do well . . . I try not to alienate an audience by talking to them in a tone that makes them feel that I'm indicting their belief or their sincerity. And that's really important when you're working with teachers, because I think, by and large, most . . . teachers get up every day trying to make sure that every child in their classroom succeeds. I don't think teachers get up in the morning to go and try to make sure that they perpetuate the achievement gap. I think they try to eliminate it. So I have to try to affirm that effort and . . . inspire them to work smarter and work harder, and . . . demonstrate that we have succeeded so that they are motivated to continue working on it. I think the worst thing that you can do is not acknowledge the success that we have achieved, because success is motivating. And if all you do is underscore the fact that we have not eliminated the gap, then I think . . . you . . . create a sense of fatalism in teachers that really does not serve children well, and underappreciates why they got into the profession to begin with.

Like Murphy, Brian Osborne was hired by a board that advertised for a new superintendent who would place a priority on narrowing achievement gaps. South Orange and Maplewood was proud of its progressive perspective on matters of social justice. Osborne saw his new community as similar in many ways to Oak Park, Illinois, where he grew up, in that they shared a history of early integration of housing.

Osborne's outlook on the achievement gap was very similar to Freeman and Murphy's, and although pushing hard for greater attention
to the achievement gap, he was nevertheless very aware of the need for
balance:

> It's an ever-evolving process. I've been front and center on the achievement
> gap since walking in the door. I've always framed it as an excellence and
> equity kind of mission we're on . . . And I'm mindful and want to be careful
> that we preserve the support and the excellence in the system that we have.
> I know . . . a lot of people . . . see it as a zero-sum game . . . and you have to
> constantly convince them that you can expand access without diluting quality
> and without diluting expectations.

Unlike Freeman, Murphy, and Osborne, Sherman believed that to accomplish his mission he needed to disrupt the Alexandria community's
vision of itself. To make progress, he thought he needed to directly and
boldly counter the myths of equity created by the "Remember the Titans" legacy, based on the integration of Alexandria's football team in
1971 and depicted in the 2000 movie of the same name starring Denzel
Washington:

> There's an interesting history which is different from any other city I've
> seen . . . [Integration] took place not around the football team but because we
> had a court order to integrate. T.C. Williams [after whom the district's single
> high school was named] was the superintendent at the time. He had been the
> superintendent for over thirty years and joined the governor in 1958 in mas-
> sive resistance to integration. That same year, he built [and] opened . . . an
> all-black school in 1958. And I know that because the mayor of the city went
> to that school. He said it was all black, and [had] smaller rooms, smaller hall-
> ways, [and] was built on a tiny postage stamp part of the city.
> [In] 1971, when there was such violence that's not shown in *Remember the
> Titans*, we had seventeen thousand kids, twelve thousand of them . . . white
> . . . By 1980 we had twelve thousand kids, four thousand of whom were white.

Sherman explained that the school boards of that time created public
documents calling for the creation of more programs for gifted and talented children to stem the tide of white flight. Instead of the heartwarm-
ing story of the integration of the Titans, Sherman's interpretation was

that ". . . rather than integration occurring, we sponsored for forty years veiled in-school segregation."

Sherman believed he needed to disabuse the community of the "Titans" myth that integration had in fact been achieved and alter the symbolic discourse of the school district and the community. He worked to do so through publishing and talking in public about disproportionality in test scores, advanced enrollments, graduation rates, extracurricular activities, and a variety of other issues. His efforts had what he termed "unanimous support" of his board, which helped him particularly after the renewal of his contract in working for change with faculties, many of whose members had initially assumed a "this too shall pass" attitude in response to his agenda. In sum, Sherman's strategy was to expose the inaccuracies in comfortable stories about Alexandria's past in order to help the community confront and address the city's legacies of racism.

A slightly different focus in communicating the work on achievement gaps was adopted by Jim Lee. When talking with Paradise Valley parents on the subject, he emphasized the instructional issues on which they were working and the difficulties less advantaged youngsters faced in learning, so that they would understand ". . . those challenges . . . and that closing the achievement gap is not an easy thing." Thus, Lee assumed the role of chief educator of his community—educating them regarding the needs of children who might otherwise have gone unnoticed.

Betty Feser's definition of achievement gaps as the distance between proficiency levels and student performance won acceptance from school board members opposed to comparing student achievement by race or assuming that white performance was the standard against which other groups' performance should be measured. Like Lee, she also focused heavily on what could be done instructionally to ensure high performance from all students. We suspect that she was looked to as the chief arbiter or mediator to help the community get over disagreements that stood in the way of progress on achievement gaps.

Each of these superintendents expressed similar visions regarding the nature of achievement gaps and shared a number of approaches to deflecting threats to that vision. With slightly different degrees of emphasis, all of them, with the exception of Sherman, stressed that they were not proposing a zero-sum game. Nor were they questioning the motives of those concerned about losing resources for their own children. Nevertheless, each of them maintained a strong stance supporting equity, thus validating the communities' own perceptions of their commitments to social justice.

CONCLUSION

Each of these superintendents faced threats directed at their work on equity related to structural, political, human resource, and symbolic factors, and each of them countered these threats using structural, political, human resource, or symbolic strategies or combinations of strategies. Structural threats such as organizational patterns encouraging each school to go its own way regardless of systemic goals were counteracted by strategic plans and policies focused on narrowing gaps, and by monitoring and evaluation consonant with those plans and policies. Diffuse curriculum and instructional procedures were replaced with coherent programming and human resources development. Personnel acting in opposition to equity goals were persuaded to follow policy or encouraged to consider working elsewhere. Rules precluding the participation of students of color in advanced educational experiences were overcome through the structural strategy of changing the rules and the human resource strategy of training. Budgets, also structural artifacts, were threatened by strong political interest groups; superintendents parried these threats by, among other things, politically astute accommodations and symbolic appeals to the communities' sense of social justice. Human resource threats such as color blindness were met by cultural competence training. Symbolic threats in the form of rejection of equity agendas were met by a combination of symbolic and political appeals implicit in how the work on opportunity and achievement gaps was portrayed.

CHAPTER EIGHT

Building from Lessons Learned

Children begin life with different opportunities to achieve their goals. The differences stem largely from the circumstances of their birth—economic status, ethnicity, country of origin, residence, and many other factors. They enter schools with the hope of learning and growing in ways that will allow them to achieve their potential. Yet achievement and other outcome data in the United States show clearly that most never leave their birth circumstances behind and for many these factors become liabilities as they move through US school systems. The superintendents whom we have profiled each embraced the ideal of schools as places of opportunity that could mitigate or eliminate constraints that might be preventing students from reaching their potential. Emphasis on potential recognizes that not all students will achieve the same results; some will inevitably be more successful than others, but efforts to close achievement and opportunity gaps involve eliminating individual and institutional bias from the equation that produces student outcomes. Framing the equity problem in terms of multiple achievement gaps, the superintendents profiled in this book worked with their boards, their communities, their leadership teams, and their teachers to craft new means of helping underserved students achieve at higher levels and graduate from high school with the potential to attend college and fully participate in the economy and society. We hope we have been clear in explaining how they approached the problems they faced and how they perceived their successes and shortcomings.

These superintendents found ways to create opportunities for students who traditionally have been excluded from the best their systems have to offer. They did it through stronger support for families, expanded early childhood education, curriculum design, inclusive policies, teacher professional development, addressing race and identity, and forcefully advocating for greater equity in their school systems. We have shown that progress was uneven and fragile, yet was evident. This final chapter uses the superintendents' experiences to reconsider how we analyze achievement gaps and efforts to close them and suggests implications for future practice and research.

ESSENTIAL QUESTIONS

We posed the fundamental question of equity-seeking educators in the introduction: *What can we do to change the educational experiences of previously underserved students so that they learn and perform at a level close or equal to those who have traditionally thrived in the US education system?* The superintendents showed us the many different ways in which they addressed this question. From their experiences, we can see what might work in other contexts, such as conducting difficult conversations about race that lead to more culturally responsive teaching, or designing specialized, ongoing advising, coaching, and support for first-generation families and students attempting to enter college after high school graduation. But we also acknowledge that not one of the superintendents made it to the finish line. No matter how long they engaged in gap-closing work, no one claimed to have closed any particular gap. These school districts that have been particularly focused on equalizing educational opportunities for their student populations have not achieved the ideal of eliminating race, poverty, disability, or language as strong predictors of educational outcomes, but they have provided important directions for how to move closer to that place on the educational map.

Deeply interested in the social justice work these men and women pursued, we posed the question, *How did you go about it?* The broad answer is that they used an organizational learning approach that drew on resources throughout their school systems and from the communities in which they were embedded. Their behaviors were consistent with organizational learning but not exactly as we originally envisioned in figure 2.1.

THE EQUITY FRAMEWORK REVISITED

Organizational learning is presented in literature as an inquiry process that can be guided by leaders, but is essentially organic in nature. In practice, we found that many of the superintendents were not content to let the organizational learning process take a natural course. Instead, they threw out old governing variables and inserted new ones, such as when Hardy Murphy eliminated pull-out approaches for students with special needs, replacing a governing variable that denied "low-expectations" children a full classroom experience with another that required high expectations and access to rigorous academic experiences for all students. Mark Freeman did the same when he declared that there would no longer be entry barriers for advanced programs. Implementing these kinds of new rules and procedures surfaced the uncomfortable reasons why the old governing variables persisted. When Sue Zurvalec, Neil Pederson, Mort Sherman, and others changed norms related to ignoring or denying racial issues, they openly expressed what few others from the inside would—that their systems were constrained by racism in many different manifestations. Often, discussing what had been undiscussable was assisted by examinations of student achievement and participation data. Publicizing data is the key in the dynamic process of clarifying why problems have persisted and changing rules and norms. The superintendents led the processes of making sense of that data through careful analysis and clarifying the results into clear problem statements that provided targets for action. At the same time, superintendents needed to make clear that they had no intention of impeaching the *motives* of people in the schools or the community.

We found that the behaviors of these superintendents closely resembled what the organizational learning literature predicts as they developed their agendas for addressing disparities in student achievement constrained by background factors. They looked at differences between aspirations and outcomes, addressed undiscussables that supported the status quo, and changed governing variables to achieve double-loop learning. They described their interventions to narrow achievement gaps as emanating from what they helped their school systems to learn. But there are two important questions: (1) Was the apparent organizational learning genuine, or was it engineered in a post hoc fashion based on what superintendents had already decided their districts needed? and (2) Was the learning single-loop or double-loop in terms of the effect on their organizations and the nature of changes made?[1] We are not confident that we can answer these questions, but we did find some clues.

Our sample of superintendents is characterized by their predisposition to engage in equity work. Their active involvement in MSAN suggests that they led change in their school districts with a belief that they needed to promote socially just educational outcomes. This vision is not something they needed to learn—but their districts did. The superintendents understood that they could not command their school districts into more equitable outcomes. Hence, they worked carefully to achieve common understandings among their varied constituencies—the community, the board, central office administrators, school site leaders, teachers, parents, and students. The superintendents had clear ideas about the directions they wanted to go, while at the same time realizing that they needed to identify like-minded educators within their systems and help others to see the instructional challenges from perspectives similar to theirs. We found no evidence that these superintendents forced or faked the outcomes associated with changing how people thought about educational goals in their districts. Thus, it seems as though organizational learning occurred. The districts these superintendents led experienced changes in approaches to education and changes in educational outcomes consistent with constituents' common understandings generated by organizational learning processes.

Figure 8.1 shows our modified conceptual framework, which takes into account what we learned about how these superintendents worked toward greater equity. In being more specific, it deviates somewhat from the literature on which it is based, but it also becomes a model that more accurately reflects what happens in practice. The superintendent vision for social justice now links directly to the governing variables they sought to change; the specific interventions they used are now part of the learning framework, as are the outcomes on which the superintendents focused. The new model also acknowledges the threats from inside and outside the system—the tensions created by change, constraints imposed by environment factors such as changes in available resources, and the general vulnerability of efforts to achieve social justice.

The thirteen superintendents were not content with one strategy. By improving practices in different ways throughout their systems, they created

FIGURE 8.1   Revised conceptual framework for pursuing educational equity.

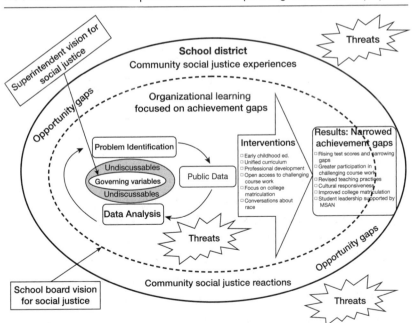

conditions for double-loop learning that have potential for long-lasting effects. A multifaceted approach that addresses pre-K, a unified curriculum, and mitigating threats arising from institutionalized racism were common targets for these superintendents and generated substantial changes in how their school districts educated children. The specific programs are of secondary importance in our analysis. We wish to emphasize key change characteristics: *Through a process of organizational learning that involved multiple constituencies, these superintendents generated families of approaches that coalesced into an overarching gap-closing strategy in their districts.*

The conceptual framework introduced in chapter 2 works reasonably well to explain the fundamental changes these superintendents fostered in their districts. The general patterns of these superintendents' intentions, interventions, and successes, strongly suggest that organizational learning did occur, which has implications for both practice and research.

ACHIEVING GREATER EQUITY IN PRACTICE

Superintendents

These superintendents clearly stood out from the field because of their longevity in the role in a single district. It is probably not possible to make substantial change for underserved students embedded in such intractable and powerful social and educational problems as poverty, racism, and inequitable distribution of resources unless a skilled superintendent addresses such challenges over an extended period of time. We recognize that this is not entirely within the superintendent's control—contracts typically run three to five years. But the political implications of extending a superintendent's tenure suggest that equity work requires managing community and board relations—and other key elements of organizational stability—to make contract renewal a matter of course, or at least of secondary importance to the board. Some of the superintendents were very frank about calculating the amount of pressure they could put on their systems without being tossed out. Underlying this practical calculation, however, is a willingness to take the long view. Superintendents who focus only on short-term results as a means of renewing contracts or advancing their careers are not likely to achieve organizational learning and the potential power of solutions that address root causes of achievement gaps. Double-loop learning requires more time than the typical contract.

An additional time factor is how schools and districts pace themselves for change. Meaningful change takes time and nurturing to become well rooted. Several of the superintendents spoke of initiatives started before their arrival, which they then sustained until they could start to see results. Too often, schools are subject to waves of changes, each one arriving before the previous one has been fully absorbed. Naturally, teachers and others become cynical under such circumstances. These superintendents worked hard to maintain focus on specific initiatives to address their equity agendas. We do not know if or how they protected their schools and the district from change initiatives or fads that were outside of their areas of focus.

Even the most long-serving superintendent's tenure in a particular district ends at some point. In the time between our interviews in 2011 and the writing of this book, several of the participating superintendents retired or moved on to new districts. We do not know if and how the equity work that was so central to their leadership continued after their departure, but wish to point out that planning for the longevity of programs is at least as important as efforts to serve as superintendent long enough to establish a sense of stability and put new governing variables in place. We are optimistic that organizational learning serves this end well. Individuals who have participated in organizational learning seem more likely to have made the interventions part of their professional identity and ongoing work as compared with those who are merely told what they must implement in classrooms. It would be interesting to test that hypothesis.

Reformers

Reform is deeply embedded in the history of US education and presents political and social challenges that have been well documented.[2] Reformers often seek a major impact on education by promoting simplistic solutions to complex problems, such as computer-based learning, zero-tolerance discipline systems, or market-driven competition. We suggest that those who wish to help close achievement gaps either from nonprofit platforms, from a policy perspective, or within public schools can learn from these superintendents' experiences.

Reformers often fail to realize that good ideas are in short supply and their effectiveness is, furthermore, context-bound and context-specific. MSAN provided a forum through which the superintendents could learn from each other's experiences and see results. The superintendents occasionally spoke of emulating one another, but when they did so, they did not, as reformers might, anoint this or that tactic as "best practice." Instead, they were interested in identifying the principles behind a particular intervention and finding ways in which those principles might be applied in a manner compatible with their current programs and processes; that is, they were more inclined to think in terms of what they had learned about their own districts to determine if and how an appealing idea might be adapted to their districts' needs. None spoke about "scaling" anything, despite the current appeal of that term to powerful educational philanthropists and some policymakers. A few national programs (such as AVID, Read 180, or the Tripod project) were widely adopted, but only as components of larger systemwide efforts. There was never one answer for these superintendents, and it would be helpful if would-be reformers could see their ostensibly good ideas in that light.

Another lesson that superintendents can teach reformers is patience. In the current era of big philanthropy frustrated with what is seen as the slow pace of education improvement, nonprofit organizations poised to help close achievement gaps are under increasing pressure to "show impact" before funding runs out. This mentality flies in the face of the thirteen superintendents' reality of measured progress, methodically pursued. No one can rush the mitigation of centuries of racism, but sustaining the effort over as much as a generation (remember Freeman's twenty-five years and Pederson's nineteen years of difficult conversations) may mean that children can be gradually liberated from the burdens of institutionalized racism. We know that philanthropists and nonprofits have to show results to justify their expenditures, but we believe they would do well to take the long view and recognize that though progress was made, achievement gaps were not closed in any of the cases presented in this book. They may be one day, but it won't be thanks to those who wish to reform public education from the outside—unless they shift their attention to helping school districts adapt their reforms in ways consonant with local conditions and combinations of extant interventions. They will need to be satisfied with approaching the elusive finish line by sustaining progress.

Principals and Teachers

These superintendents clearly viewed principals as critical members of their leadership teams. Although they did not go into specifics, several spoke of the importance of principals in promoting the equity agenda. For example, Bill Lupini and Neil Pederson emphasized that part of their success was due to having hired all, or nearly all, of the principals working in their systems.

The professional relationship between superintendents and principals can be difficult, at least in part because of superintendents' dependence on principals to implement their agendas. Principals have the stress of living hour-by-hour and day-by-day with the fallout from change. Equity efforts are particularly fraught with discontent among teachers, parents, and students. Thus, principals may be tempted to soft-pedal superintendents' social justice agendas to maintain peace in their schools.

Our interviews clearly indicate that planned, systemic change was critical to progress in narrowing achievement gaps. Principals likely agree with superintendents' equity agendas and are perceived as crucial participants in the school system. Thus, we encourage principals to embrace their instructional leadership roles and their power to shape school cultures to make the best of what their schools have to offer available in equal measure to all students. As mid-level leaders, principals face pressures from a number of sources, but they also have substantial power to shape their schools and their schools' messages to families. They can work for greater equity while maintaining challenging, high-quality programs for the most talented students and students in the middle. These superintendents clearly wanted that kind of balancing act from their principals.

Teachers make educational equity happen. But like principals, they may be reluctant to upset the status quo. Teachers risk a lot when they begin to change their practice. Anyone who has taught understands this problem. When faced with large numbers of students, any one of whom on any given day is fully capable of disrupting learning, change from tried-and-true practices is hard. The problem of classroom stability, coupled with a need to please students and their parents, was a likely source of the resistance Freeman and others faced when they cleared away barriers to entering classrooms with the most challenging curricula. When the superintendents were able to assist teachers with meaningful professional development to handle different mixes of students in their classrooms, teachers often embraced open access to the most challenging courses, especially when they saw how successful they could be. Teachers should insist on professional development that gives them the skills and knowledge to teach more diverse classrooms, and when they get it, we hope they will run with it in the effort to improve outcomes for underserved students.

RESEARCH PATHWAYS

There are many questions we were unable to answer because of the limitations of our methods and the scope of a single volume. Now that the superintendents' voices have been heard on the issue of gap-closing in pursuit of education equity, three questions that merit further examination come into clearer focus.

To What Extent Does Organizational Learning Occur, and How Deeply Does It Penetrate in the Organization?

We are struck by the differing realities of people in different places within a school system. For example, values and beliefs held by superintendents and their cabinets may be very different from those espoused by teachers, despite the hierarchical nature of school districts. Thus, a superintendent addressing undiscussables and changing governing variables may not know who actually understands and accepts that change is happening. Even if implementation of a particular program or initiative seems uniform and widespread, one would have to be inside classrooms—possibly witnessing one-on-one interactions with students—to know if something as subtle as high expectations is being communicated. Rules, norms, and goals that seem clear in discussion are not always evident in practice.

It might be instructive for researchers to identify a small set of key governing variables, then search for evidence of them at work in schools and classrooms. One that seems particularly challenging is cultural responsiveness. If a school district such as Chapel Hill-Carrboro City has put substantial effort into confronting racial issues with the intent of making learning more accessible to all students by developing and sustaining culturally responsive teaching, then it makes sense to observe classrooms throughout the district to determine the extent to which students are exposed to culturally responsive teaching, and also its effect. Quantitative and qualitative indicators might reveal, for example, greater minority student participation in the most rigorous curriculum and more positive academic self-image among those students.

Given the importance of addressing the underlying assumptions and biases that impede the process of changing governing variables and engaging in double-loop learning, we suggest investigation into how school districts confront such undiscussables. Argyris' case study work provides guidance into how to conduct such research.[3] Case studies would allow researchers to identify the extent to which teachers, administrators, and board members align their talk and behaviors (theories in use) with the district's equity agenda, and when aspirations and outcomes are out of alignment, the extent to which the district's organization culture allows for frank discussion of why this is so.

Revealing evidence of organizational learning in the daily practice of educators demonstrates the capacity that districts and schools have to mitigate inequities in public schools. This kind of research indicates the high potential for using theory and research to inform practice, but it requires labor-intensive study of schools and districts on an intimate level possible only through mixed quantitative and qualitative methods.

How Strong Is the Link Between Interventions and Gap Narrowing?

This question essentially addresses the general theory of action promoted by participating superintendents: understand the nature and extent of achievement gaps based on outcomes data, learn the causes of these gaps, then target interventions that will mitigate the causes and reduce the gaps. But maybe it's not that simple. Was it Bill Lupini's after-school support in Brookline's housing projects that positively affected college matriculation for this portion of the school district's population? Or was the effort to provide access to rigorous instruction the most important factor, with tutoring in the projects simply meeting an academic need not previously addressed? Causal research, such as the component-building approach advocated by Slavin, might help to identify the most powerful factors that narrow different kinds of gaps, informing school districts about efficient resource allocation. (Slavin suggests the identification of a series of interventions, or components—in our case, such components would be the separate interventions discussed by the superintendents. Then, in a given study, a component could be dropped to discover the impact of its absence in one setting and compare that result to the full complement in another setting or settings. Additional studies would test the dropping of different components.[4]) We strongly suspect that interventions support each other—i.e., each alone is weaker than all collectively—and that they therefore need to be studied together.

Yet the interventions are not always stable, quantifiable inputs. Unifying the curriculum was common across several school districts, but we do not know much about what the elementary curriculum in each case looked like and whether it was well aligned with challenging courses at the secondary level. Thus, qualitative research that illuminates the nature of the curriculum offered, the pedagogy acquired through professional development, and the degree to which early student experiences prepare students for what comes later would help to evaluate how schools and districts enhance (or not) minority students' learning as they progress through the grades. It is as important to know *how* the outcomes were achieved as it is to know what caused the outcomes.

Do the Benefits of Gap-Narrowing Persist Beyond High School Graduation?

As the superintendents' experiences have shown, social justice work in education requires reallocation of resources to achieve results. Justifying extended early childhood programs, teacher professional development focused on delivering a unified curriculum, or more sections of AP courses naturally leads to discussion of the benefits resulting from such efforts. One could argue that higher-quality educational experiences are important ends in themselves so that students can grow into adults who understand their world and how to thrive in it. But policymakers, parents, and school officials seem to seek more concrete benefits to education. Not all agree on how these ought to be defined, but there appears to be substantial emphasis on college matriculation and persistence as a measure of pre-K–12 educational quality.

The growing importance of a college degree for participation in the contemporary workforce suggests the significance behind determining how well equity interventions improve persistence in college. In addition to learning the effectiveness of such interventions, this type of research might also help to reveal the relative power of opportunity gaps and achievement gaps and the extent to which each can be mitigated by actions taken within school systems.

A WORD ABOUT METHOD

As quantitative data sets become richer and more extensive within a more data-driven culture fostered by years of calls for accountability, and as quantitative methods powered by more sophisticated software reveal connections and causation that could not have been previously discovered, the value of qualitative inquiry may get lost in the excitement. We agree with Maxwell and others that quantitative methods tell us what happened, but not how and why it happened.[5] A systemic approach to research on how achievement gaps are narrowed based on the concepts embedded in organizational learning yields quantitative outcomes that are informative but incomplete without an understanding of how and why they were achieved.

We advocate a mixed methods approach to future inquiry into gap-closing efforts aimed at achieving greater social justice because some of the outcomes are not amenable to measure—such as the mechanisms by which participation in extracurricular activities closes gaps in student achievement and promotes social justice—and because understanding the "how" and "why" of gap closing is at least as important as understanding the evidence that indeed one or more gaps have narrowed. Answers to how and why questions help to point the way forward for districts not yet successful in addressing gaps, to the benefit of greater numbers of students.

FINAL THOUGHTS

We deeply admire the superintendents represented in this volume for their dedication to providing disadvantaged students with far better educational opportunities than others like them enjoyed in earlier generations. We also respect their talents, values, work ethic, persistence, and resilience. All of these personal qualities are undoubtedly requirements for engaging in the challenging, complex, and ambiguous effort to equalize educational opportunity so that important educational outcomes are not reliably predicted by race, poverty, home language, or disability. We hope, however, that our esteem for these superintendents has not colored the narrative to the extent that credibility is compromised. More important, we do not wish to convey that the kind of leadership depicted here is unattainable by most of the rest of us. On the contrary, it is our aspiration that by organizing these superintendents' disparate efforts into common themes, we have shown readers promising pathways for narrowing achievement gaps in the diversity of settings that make up the US education system.

It is probably true that too much is expected of public education in the United States—from teaching children how to maintain their health to preparing them for jobs and careers that don't even exist yet—and that much of the discourse focused on school success or failure serves political rather than educational ends. Yet we must not lose sight of the fact that children go to school to learn—for whatever purpose we may impose on that learning. If we start from the premise that tax-supported public education should serve all students equally well, then as ethical educators we have no choice but to find ways to eliminate student background factors as predictors of their achievement. The ideal may be impossible to achieve, but the experiences of the thirteen superintendents represented here suggest that we are only just beginning to learn what to do. We hope their example will inspire others to stay the course toward the ideal.

APPENDIX A: Enrollment and Percentage by Race/Ethnicity of Participating MSAN Districts: 2011–2012 School Year

District	Enrolled (N)	Native American	Asian	Black	Latino	Pacific Islander	Multi-racial	White
					Percent by race/ethnicity			
Alexandria	12,396	0.01	5	34	30	0	2	28
Arlington	21,859	0	9	11	28	0	5	47
Bedford	4,425	0	4	4	24	0	2	65
Brookline	7,224	0	2	7	10	0	8	58
Chapel Hill-Carrboro City	11,885	0.01	15	12	14	0	7	52
Evanston-Skokie	7,352	0	5	27	20	0	7	41
Farmington	11,435	0	12	26	2	0	2	57
Madison	25,011	0	9	19	18	0	8	45
Paradise Valley	31,500	0.01	3	3	25	0	3	63
Princeton	3,503	0	17	7	11	0	4	63
Shaker Heights	5,338	0	4	50	2	0	6	38
South Orange and Maplewood	6,532	0	4	39	4	0	4	48
Windsor	3,613*	0	5	48	14	0	3	30
Total	152,073	0	8	17	19	0	5	50

*2010–2011.

APPENDIX B: Enrollment and Percentage of English Language Learners, Special Education Students, and Recipients of Subsidized Meals and Per-Pupil Costs of Participating MSAN Districts: 2011–2012 School Year

District	Enrolled (N)	ELL	SPED	Free and reduced-price lunch	Per-pupil cost*
Alexandria	12,396	28	13	53	$17,618
Arlington	21,859	17	15	31	18,047
Bedford	4,425	7	9	15	26,063
Brookline	7,224	9	17	12	16,556
Chapel Hill-Carrboro City	11,885	11	12	25	10,548
Evanston-Skokie	7,352	11	12	40	14,661
Farmington	11,435	23	12	24	12,327
Madison	25,011	19	14	50	13,493
Paradise Valley	31,500	5	13	43	5,600
Princeton	3,503	3	13	12	18,279
Shaker Heights	5,338	2	14	34	15,875
South Orange and Maplewood	6,532	1	13	19	17,905
Windsor	3,613**	3	13	28	11,545
Total	152,073	13	13	36	15,540***

*Compiled 2012–2013 from district websites.

**2010–2011.

***Mean.

APPENDIX C: Participating Superintendents' Past and Current Positions

Superintendent	MSAN District	Years of service	Current (2015)
Feser, Elizabeth	Windsor Public Schools (CT)	2002–2011	Superintendent, Milford Public Schools (CT)
Freeman, Mark	Shaker Heights Schools (OH)*	1988–2013	Executive in Residence at Cleveland State University
Hochman, Jere	Amherst-Pelham Regional School District (MA)*	2003–2008	Deputy Secretary of Education, New York State
	Bedford Central School District (NY)	2008–2015	
Lee, Jim	Paradise Valley Unified School District (AZ)*	2009–Present	
Lupini, Bill	Brookline Public Schools (MA)*	2004–2015	Interim Superintendent, Essex Technical High School (Danvers, MA)
Murphy, Hardy	Evanston/Skokie School District 65 (IL)*	1999–2012	Research scientist/scholar, Indiana University School of Education
Murphy, Patrick	Arlington Public Schools (VA)*	2009–present	
Nerad, Daniel	Green Bay Area Public School District (WI)	2001–2008	Superintendent, Birmingham Public Schools (MI)*
	Madison Metropolitan School District (WI)*	2008–2012	
Osborne, Brian	The School District of South Orange and Maplewood (NJ)*	2007–2014	Superintendent, City School District of New Rochelle (NY)
Pederson, Neil	Chapel Hill-Carrboro City Schools (NC)*	1992–2011	Executive Director of the Central Carolina Regional Education Service Alliance, Raleigh (NC)
Sherman, Morton	Cherry Hill Public Schools (NJ)	1997–2005	Associate Executive Director, American Association of School Administrators
	Alexandria City Public Schools (VA)*	2008–2013	
Wilson, Judy	Princeton Public Schools (NJ)*	2005–2013	Consultant at Judith Ives Wilson, LLC
Zurvalec, Susan	Farmington Public Schools (MI)*	2005–2014	HR consultant, executive coach

*MSAN districts as of 2015.

Notes

Introduction

1. Katherine Magnuson and Jane Waldfogel, eds., *Steady Gains and Stalled Progress: Inequality and the Black-White Test Score Gap* (New York: Russell Sage Foundation, 2008); Richard Rothstein, *Class and Schools: Using Social, Economic, and Educational Reform to Close the Black-White Achievement Gap* (Washington, DC: Economic Policy Institute, 2004); and Thomas B. Timar and Julie Maxell-Jolly, eds., *Narrowing the Achievement Gap: Perspectives and Strategies for Challenging Times* (Cambridge, MA: Harvard Education Press, 2012).
2. National Center for Education Statistics, "Digest of Education Statistics," Institute of Education Sciences, https://nces.ed.gov/programs/digest/d12/tables/dt12_098.asp.
3. Robert G. Smith et al., *Gaining on the Gap: Changing Hearts, Minds and Practice* (Lanham, MD: Rowman & Littlefield, 2011).
4. David D. Berliner, *Poverty and Potential: Out-of-School Factors and School Success* (Boulder and Tempe: Education and the Public Interest Center & Education Policy Research Unit, 2009) Retrieved from http://epicpolicy.org/publication/poverty-and-potential; Wade Boykin and Pedro Noguera, *Creating the Opportunity to Learn: Moving Research to Practice to Close the Achievement Gap* (Alexandria, VA: ASCD, 2011); Jeffrey S. Brooks, *Black School, White School: Racism and Educational (Mis)Leadership* (New York: Teachers College Press, 2012); Stacey M. Childress, Denis P. Doyle, and David A. Thomas, *Leading for Equity: The Pursuit of Excellence in Montgomery County Public Schools* (Cambridge, MA: Harvard Education Press, 2009); Ronald F. Ferguson, *Toward Excellence with Equity: An Emerging Vision for Closing the Achievement Gap* (Cambridge, MA: Harvard Education Press, 2007); Christopher Jencks and Meredith Phillips, *The Black-White Test Score Gap* (Washington, DC: The Brookings Institution, 1998); Magnuson and Waldfogel, *Steady Gains*; Richard Rothstein, *Class and Schools*; Smith et al., *Gaining on the Gap*; Timar and Maxell-Jolly, *Narrowing the Achievement Gap*; David S. Yeager and Gregory M. Walton, "Social Psychological Interventions in Education: They're Not Magic," *Review of Educational Research* 81 (2011): 267–301.
5. Smith et al., *Gaining on the Gap*.

6. Ibid.; Chris Argyris, *On Organizational* Learning, 2nd ed. (Malden, MA: Blackwell Publishing, 1999), 151–163; Chris Argyris and Donald Schön, *Theory in Practice: Increasing Professional Effectiveness* (San Francisco: Jossey-Bass, 1974); and Chris Argyris and Donald Schön, *Organizational Learning: A Theory of Action Perspective* (Reading, MA: Addison-Wesley, 1978).

7. Barney G. Glaser and Anselm L. Strauss, *The Discovery of Grounded Theory: Strategies for Qualitative Research* (New Brunswick, NJ: Aldine Transaction, 1967), 101–116; and Joseph A. Maxwell, *Qualitative Research Design: An Interactive Approach* (Thousand Oaks, CA: Sage Publications, 1996), 77, 79, 95–96.

8. Sharan B. Merriman, *Qualitative Research: A Guide to Design and Implementation* (San Francisco: Jossey-Bass, 2009), 223–228; and Robert K. Yin, *Case Study Research: Design and Methods*, 2nd ed. (Thousand Oaks, CA: Sage Publications); Matthew B. Miles and Michael Huberman, *Qualitative Data Analysis: An Expanded Sourcebook*, 2nd ed. (Thousand Oaks, CA: Sage Publications), 29; and Yin, *Case Study Research*.

9. Christopher A. Lubienski and Sarah Theule Lubienski, *The Public School Advantage: Why Public Schools Outperform Private Schools* (Chicago: University of Chicago Press, 2013) Joshua D. Angrist, Parag A. Pathak, and Christopher R. Walters, *Charter School Performance in California* (Center for Research on Education Outcomes, Stanford University, Stanford, CA, 2014).

10. Richard F. Elmore, *School Reform from the Inside Out: Policy, Practice, and Performance* (Cambridge, MA: Harvard Education Press, 2004), 211–226.

11. Lee G. Bolman and Terrence E. Deal, *Reframing Organizations: Artistry, Choice, and Leadership*, 5th ed. (San Francisco: Jossey-Bass, 2013.

Chapter 1

1. Robert G. Smith et al., *Gaining on the Gap: Changing Hearts, Minds and Practice* (Lanham, MD: Rowman & Littlefield, 2011),

2. Allan Alson, "The Minority Student Achievement Network," *Educational Leadership* 60 (2003): 76–78.

3. MSAN, "Minority Student Achievement Network: Organizational Plan" (unpublished document, Minority Student Achievement Network, 2000), 2.

4. Ibid., 4–5.

5. Ibid., 4.

6. Ibid.,9.

7. Robert G. Smith and Stephanie L. Knight, "The University of Houston School-University Research Collaborative," (paper presented at the annual meeting of the American Educational Research Association, Atlanta, GA, April 1993).

8. Laura A. Cooper, "Why Closing the Research-Practice Gap Is Critical to Closing Student Achievement Gaps," *Theory into Practice* 46 (2007): 317–324.

9. Ibid.

10. http://tripoded.com; Ronald F. Ferguson, *Toward Excellence with Equity: An Emerging Vision for Closing the Achievement Gap* (Cambridge, MA: Harvard Education

Press, 2007), 5–6. The Tripod project is a professional development model based on sharing with teachers student feedback regarding their experiences with instruction and their relationships with their teachers. This information was used to try to improve what Ferguson called the three "legs" of effective education—pedagogy, instruction, and relationships.

11. "Research-Practitioner Council," June 2015, http://msan.wceruw.org/about/board-council.html.

12. MSAN, "Organizational Plan," 4, 7.

13. Robert G. Smith and S. David Brazer, "Achievement Gaps and Superintendent Decisions," (paper presented at the annual meeting of the American Educational Research Association, San Francisco, CA, April 2013).

14. Conference agenda, 2015 MSAN Institute, June 2015, http://msan.wceruw.org/conferences/institute2015.html.

15. Jon Campbell, "Bedford Schools Chief to Be Deputy Education Secretary" *LOLHUD The Journal News*, October 28, 2015, http://www.lohud.com/story/news/education/2015/10/28/jere-hochman-cuomo/74744344/.

16. Arizona School Boards Association, "Breaking the Piggy Bank: Arizona Education," 2015, http://www.azsba.org/wp-content/uploads/2015/06/Untitled-Infographic41.pdf.

17. Dave Rattigan, "Brookline administrator tabbed as Essex Tech superintendent," *Boston Globe*, September 29, 2015 https://www.bostonglobe.com/metro/regionals/north/2015/09/29/brookline-administrator-tabbed-essex-tech-superintendent/l9Y1hhVLJAfpLdPt9yX5MO/story.html.

18. http://www.iidc.indiana.edu/index.php?pageId=directory&mode=mod_md&action=display_detail&md_id=90.

Chapter 2

1. Chris Argyris, *On Organizational* Learning, 2nd ed. (Malden, MA: Blackwell Publishing, 1999), 4–14; Chris Argyris and Donald Schön, *Theory in Practice: Increasing Professional Effectiveness* (San Francisco: Jossey-Bass, 1974), 37–136; and Chris Argyris and Donald Schön, *Organizational Learning: A Theory of Action Perspective* (Reading, MA: Addison-Wesley, 1978); Debra Ingram, Karen Seashore Louis, and Roger G. Schroeder, "Accountability Policies and Teacher Decision Making: Barriers to the Use of Data to Improve Practice," *Teachers College Record* 106 (2004): 1258–1262.

2. Kenneth Leithwood, Alma Harris, and David Hopkins, "Seven Strong Claims About Successful School Leadership," *School Leadership and Management* 28 (2008): 29–31.

3. See, for example, Michelle D. Van Lare and S. David Brazer, "Analyzing Learning in Professional Learning Communities," *Leadership and Policy in Schools* 12 (2013): 374–396, doi: 10.1080/15700763.2013.860463.

4. Argyris and Schön, *Theory in Practice*, 6–7; 29–30.

5. Ibid., 141–144.

6. Paul J. DiMaggio and Walter W. Powell, "The Iron Cage Revisited: Institutional Isomorphism and Collective Rationality in Organizational Fields," *American Sociological Review* 48 (1983): 148–155.
7. Argyris and Schön, *Theory in Practice*, 18–19.
8. Ibid., 18–19, 24.
9. Ibid., 86–89, 102–103.
10. Robert G. Smith et al., *Gaining on the Gap: Changing Hearts, Minds and Practice* (Lanham, MD: Rowman & Littlefield, 2011), 21–27.
11. Leithwood, Harris, and Hopkins, "Seven Strong Claims," 29–32.
12. Smith et al., *Gaining on the Gap*, 35–40.
13. Prudence L. Carter and Kevin G. Welner, *Closing the Opportunity Gap: What America Must Do to Give Every Child an Even Chance* (Oxford: Oxford University Press, 2013).

Chapter 3

1. The term *minority student* is somewhat awkward because of racial and ethnic connotations. We use the term to capture all students who do not typically constitute the majority population in suburban districts, including non-white races, non-Anglo-Saxon ethnicities, students with disabilities, students living in poverty, and students whose first language is not English.
2. Chris Argyris and Donald Schön, *Theory in Practice: Increasing Professional Effectiveness* (San Francisco: Jossey-Bass, 1974), 37–136.
3. James G. March, *A Primer on Decision Making* (New York: The Free Press, 1994), 181–186.
4. http://ipistudentengagement.com.
5. Robert G. Smith et al., *Gaining on the Gap: Changing Hearts, Minds and Practice* (Lanham, MD: Rowman & Littlefield, 2011), 21–27.
6. Argyris and Schön, *Theory in Practice*, 63–109.
7. Chris Argyris, *On Organizational Learning*, 2nd ed. (Malden, MA: Blackwell Publishing, 1999), 19–91; 239–266.
8. Argyris and Schön, *Theory in Practice*, 85–95.

Chapter 4

1. Larry Cuban, *The Managerial Imperative and the Practice of Leadership in Schools* (Albany: State University of New York Press, 1988), 111–112.
2. Paul W. Lawrence and Jay W. Lorsch, "Differentiation and Integration in Complex Organizations," *Administrative Science Quarterly* 12 (1967): 1–47.
3. Robert G. Smith et al., *Gaining on the Gap: Changing Hearts, Minds and Practice* (Lanham, MD: Rowman & Littlefield, 2011), 43–46.

Chapter 5

1. Michael S. Knapp, "Professional Development as a Policy Pathway," *Review of Research in Education* 27 (2003): 109–155.

2. http://everydaymath.uchicago.edu.

3. http://www.beattheoddsinstitute.org.

4. Jim Collins, *Good to Great: Why Some Companies Make the Leap . . . and Others Don't* (New York: HarperCollins, 2001).

5. Mary J. Waits et al., *Why Some Schools with Latino Children Beat the Odds . . . and Others Don't* (Tempe, AZ: Morrison Institute for Public Policy and the Center for the Future of Arizona, 2006), http://www.beattheoddsinstitute.org/pdf/FAZ502_LatinEd_final.pdf.

6. The practices were: "clear bottom line" (focusing on individual classroom and individual teacher results); "ongoing assessment" (going beyond standardized test scores); "strong and steady principal" (behaviors that are flexible, yet focused on improvement); "collaborative solutions" (responsibility for solutions to instructional problems distributed to teaching teams); "stick with the program" selected by collaborative teams; and "built to suit" (programs designed for each individual child).

7. "What Is AVID?" http://www.avid.org/what-is-avid.ashx.

8. "The Read 180 Experience," http://www.scholastic.com/read180/read-180-experience/reading-program-design.htm.

9. http://tripoded.com; Ronald F. Ferguson. *Toward Excellence with Equity: An Emerging Vision for Closing the Achievement Gap* (Cambridge, MA: Harvard Education Press, 2008), 5, 225–293.

10. http://siop.pearson.com; http://tc.readingandwritingproject.com/workshops-study-groups/tc-workshops.html; Charlotte A. Danielson, *Enhancing Professional Practice: A Framework for Teaching*, 2nd ed. (Alexandria, VA: ASCD, 2007).

11. Knapp, "Professional Development."

12. Vicki Vescio, et al., "A Review of Research on the Impact of Professional Learning Communities on Teaching Practice and Student Learning," *Teaching and Teacher Education* 24 (2008): 80–91; Matthew Ronfeldt et al., "Teacher Collaboration in Instructional Teams and Student Achievement," *American Educational Research Journal* 52 (2015): 475–514.

13. Elizabeth A. City, et al., *Instructional Rounds in Education: A Network Approach to Improving Teaching and Learning* (Cambridge, MA: Harvard Education Press, 2009).

14. Robert G. Smith, "Gaining on the Gap," *School Administrator* 67 (2010): 21–24.

15. Knapp, "Professional Development."

16. Glenn Singleton, *Courageous Conversations About Race* (Thousand Oaks, CA: Corwin, 2005), 16, 17.

17. Ibid., 14–15, 32–33, 130–31.

18. Smith et al., *Gaining on the Gap*, 9–101, 153–161.

19. Derald Wing Sue et al., "Racial Microaggresions in Everyday Life: Implications for Clinical Practice," *American Psychologist* 62 (2007): 271–286.

Chapter 6

1. Prudence L. Carter and Kevin G. Welner, "Achievement Gaps Arise from Opportunity Gaps," in *Closing the Opportunity Gap*, ed. Prudence L. Carter and Kevin G. Welner (New York: Oxford University Press, 2015), 1–3.

2. Gloria Ladson Billings, "From the Achievement Gap to the Education Debt: Understanding Achievement in U.S. Schools," *Educational Researcher* 35 (2006): 1–10.

3. James S. Coleman et al., *Equality of Educational Opportunity* (Washington, DC: US Government Printing Office, 1966), 22.

4. Christopher Jencks et al., *Inequality: A Reassessment of the Effect of Family on Schooling in America* (New York: Basic Books, 1972).

5. Richard Rothstein, *Class and Schools: Using Social, Economic, and Educational Reform to Close the Black-White Achievement Gap* (Washington, DC: Economic Policy Institute, 2004), 14.

6. David C. Berliner, "Effects of Inequality and Poverty vs. Teachers and Schooling on America's Youth," *Teachers College Record* 115, (2013): 1–26.

7. Robert D. Putnam, *Our Kids: The American Dream in Crisis* (New York: Simon & Schuster, 2015), 182–183.

8. Robert G. Smith et al., *Gaining on the Gap: Changing Hearts, Minds and Practice* (Lanham, MD: Rowman and Littlefield, 2011), 49.

9. Berliner, "Effects of Inequality and Poverty," 1–26; David D. Berliner, *Poverty and Potential: Out-of-School Factors and School Success* (Boulder, CO, and Tempe, AZ: Education and the Public Interest Center & Education Policy Research Unit, 2009), http://epicpolicy.org/publication/poverty-and-potential; Carter and Welner, "Achievement Gaps Arise," 1–3; Rothstein, *Class and Schools*, 14.

10. Berliner, *Poverty and Potential*, 38; Rothstein, *Class and School*, 123–126; W. Steven Barnett and Cynthia E. Lamy, "Achievement Gaps Start Early: Preschool Can Help," in *Closing the Opportunity Gap*, 101–109.

11. Henry G. Herrod, "Do First Years Really Last a Lifetime?" *Clinical Pediatrics* 46 (2007): 199–205; Damon E. Jones, Mark Greenburg, and Max Crowley, "Early Social-Emotional Functioning and Public Health: The Relationship Between Kindergarten Social Competence and Future Wellness," *American Journal of Public Health* (Published online ahead of print July 16, 2015), http://ajph.aphapublications.org/, doi:10.2105/AJPH.2015.302630.

12. Herrod, "Do First Years Really Last a Lifetime?"

13. Fred M. Newmann, BetsAnn Smith, Elaine Allensworth, and Anthony S. Bryk, "Instructional Program Coherence: What It Is and Why It Should Guide School Improvement Policy," *Educational Evaluation and Policy Analysis* 23 (2001): 297–321.

14. Robert E. Slavin, "Mastery Learning Reconsidered," *Review of Educational Research* 57 (1987):. 175–213.

15. Robert G. Smith, "Gaining on the Gap," *School Administrator* 67 (2010): 21–24.

16. Ibid.

17. Ibid.
18. Geneva Gay, "Teaching To and Through Cultural Diversity," *Curriculum Inquiry* 43 (2013): 48–70.
19. National Student Clearing House Research Center, http://nscresearchcenter.org/.
20. George Mason University Early Identification Program, "What We Do," http://eip.gmu.edu/about-us-2/whatwedo/.
21. "Metco Program," Massachusetts Department of Education, http://www.doe.mass.edu/metco/.

Chapter 7

1. Lee. G. Bolman and Terrence E. Deal, *Reframing Organizations: Artistry, Choice, and Leadership* (San Francisco: Jossey-Bass, 2013), 3–22.
2. Ibid., 41–42.
3. Robert G. Smith et al., *Gaining on the Gap: Changing Hearts, Minds and Practice* (Lanham, MD: Rowman and Littlefield, 2011), 21–28.
4. Bolman and Deal, *Reframing Organizations*, 183–184.
5. Ibid., 113.
6. Glenn Singleton and Curtis Linton, *Courageous Conversations About Race: A Field Guide for Achieving Equity in Schools* (Thousand Oaks, CA: Corwin Press, 2006), 14–15, 32–3, 130–131.
7. Kerri Ullicci and Dan Battey, "Exposing Color Blindness / Exposing Color Consciousness," *Urban Education* 46 (2011): 1195–1225, doi: 10.1177/0042085911413150.
8. Peggy McIntosh, "White Privilege: Unpacking the Invisible Knapsack," *Independent School* 49 (1990): 1–5; Tim Wise, *White Like Me: Reflections on Race from a Privileged Son* (Brooklyn, NY: Soft Skull Press, 2011), 1–14.
9. Smith, et al., *Gaining on the Gap*, 85–146.
10. Claude M. Steele, *Whistling Vivaldi: How Stereotypes Affect Us and What We Can Do* (New York: W.W. Norton & Co., 2010), 1–62; David S. Yeager and Gregory M. Walton, "Social-Psychological Interventions in Education: They're Not Magic," *Review of Educational Research* 81 (2011), 267–301, doi: 10.3102/00346543114059.
11. "Celebrating 2015 Words Out Loud: Black Lives Matter," *The Achiever Newsletter* (Arlington, VA: Arlington Public Schools, Spring 2015).
12. Bolman and Deal, *Reframing Organizations*, 244.

Chapter 8

1. Chris Argyris and Donald Schön, *Theory in Practice: Increasing Professional Effectiveness* (San Francisco: Jossey-Bass, 1974), 63–95.
2. See for example, Larry Cuban, "Reforming Again, and Again, and Again," *Educational Researcher* 19 (1): 3–13; David Labaree, *Someone Has to Fail: The Zero-Sum Game of Public Schooling* (Cambridge, MA: Harvard University Press. 2012); David

Tyack and Larry Cuban, *Tinkering Toward Utopia* (Cambridge, MA: Harvard University Press, 1995).

3. Chris Argyris, *On Organizational* Learning, 2nd ed. (Malden, MA: Blackwell Publishing, 1999).

4. Robert E. Slavin, "A Strategy for Research-Based Instructional Improvement," *Elementary School Journal* 84 (1984): 255–269.

5. Maxwell, *Qualitative Research Design: An Interactive Approach*, 3rd ed. (Thousand Oaks, CA: Sage Publications, 2013); Merriam, *Qualitative Research: A Guide to Design and Implementation*, 3rd ed. (San Francisco: Jossey-Bass, 2009).

Acknowledgments

We extend our gratitude to the thirteen superintendents who took the time to talk with us and forthrightly shared the experiences that constitute the substance of this book. We are also indebted to Nancy Walser, our Harvard Education Press editor, who improved the book by asking penetrating questions, suggesting reorganization of material, pushing us to more clearly express our thinking, and generally providing helpful feedback. We, of course, are responsible for any of the volume's inadequacies.

About the Authors

Robert G. Smith is currently an associate professor in the George Mason College of Education and Human Development's Education Leadership program. He retired from preK–12 public education in 2009 after forty-four years in the field. He worked as a teacher, building administrator, and central office administrator, concluding his public school career after twelve years as the superintendent of the Arlington (Virginia) Public Schools. His research interests include school and school district leadership, opportunity and achievement gaps, collaborative inquiry, and teaching for meaning. Smith is coauthor, with Arlington colleagues, of *Gaining on the Gap: Changing Hearts, Minds and Practice* and has authored or coauthored a number of book chapters, as well as articles appearing in publications such as *Harvard Education Letter, Journalism Quarterly, High School Journal, Public Administration Quarterly, Equity and Excellence in Education, School Administrator*, and *Reading Today*. Smith earned his PhD at the University of Maryland, College Park.

S. David Brazer is an associate professor and Director of the Leadership Degree Programs in the Stanford University Graduate School of Education. Brazer spent fifteen years as a middle and high school teacher and administrator, serving during the last six years of his K–12 career as a high school principal. His primary research interests include decision making in schools and districts, school improvement, instructional leadership and teacher collaborative teams, and leadership preparation. He teaches leadership seminars and courses in the Policy, Organization, and Leadership Studies and joint MA/MBA programs. His recent theoretical and empirical publications have appeared in *Educational Administration Quarterly*, *Leadership and Policy in Schools*, and various edited volumes. He is the second author (with Scott Bauer) of *Using Research to Lead School Improvement: Turning Evidence into Action* (2012, Sage Publications). Brazer received his PhD from Stanford University.

Index